3-15-55

# CO-OPERATIVES
## THE BRITISH ACHIEVEMENT

# CO-OPERATIVES

## THE BRITISH ACHIEVEMENT

By PAUL GREER

*Foreword by* Lord Williams
*Introduction by* Marquis W. Childs

HARPER & BROTHERS PUBLISHERS

NEW YORK

*To my Amelia*
*a wife and mother who has made her family,*
*like a co-operative, a bridge between*
*selfish human nature and social responsibility.*

888441

# CONTENTS

# FOREWORD

By Lord Williams
*President of the Co-operative Wholesale Society*

PRODUCTION in the world today is largely well organised and well able to look after its own interests. Consumers are mostly unorganised, and many governments, notably that of the United States, have elaborate codes of law to protect the consumer from exploitation. Valuable as these safeguards are, it is difficult for them to do more than deal with the most flagrant cases.

In Great Britain, consumers have had their own organisation for well over a hundred years. The British co-operative movement consists mainly of ordinary families combining to buy and make their own day-to-day household needs. It has grown until today half the families in the country contain a co-operative member. In this way they have erected their own bulwarks against monopoly and exploitation and they ensure that production is carried on as a service to the consumer and not as a means of creating personal wealth.

I welcome the interest of Mr. Paul Greer in our achievement and our problems. Although American conditions differ from ours, I shall be happy if our experience can in any way help consumers in the United States to organise more effectively.

# INTRODUCTION

## By Marquis W. Childs

THIS is a book in many respects long overdue. It is the story told in thorough and careful detail of what the British have done through their co-operatives. It is above all a lesson in responsibility with particular meaning for us in America today.

There is scarcely a shred of the illusion left that the anti-trust laws can curb the power of the great corporations. The tendency is at an ever accelerated pace toward concentration of control in a few giant corporations. The danger is that when there are only two or three giants left, government will take over and we shall exchange the relatively efficient bureaucracy of corporate gigantism for the static bureaucracy of government. Mr. Greer tells how consumers in Great Britain have through a period of more than a century taken over the ownership and management of a considerable segment of the economy. They have done this by the democratic process which means constant and patient effort and attention to what is everybody's business.

Here are the idealism and the inspiration and also the politics of a movement that has entered actively into the political arena. Far more perhaps than any other co-operative group in the world the British co-operators are ideologically conscious. They have developed an extensive educational system which culminates in a co-operative college at Stanford Hall. Its courses on co-operative subjects are credited toward a diploma in Social Sciences by Nottingham University. Co-operators sit in the House of Commons to represent a movement that has for many of its participants both political and economic implications.

But much of the story is of the hard day-to-day work by thousands of loyal and devoted men and women in running a vast and varied enterprise. To many Americans accustomed to the neon and chromium and piped-in music of the supermarkets, this will seem grubby and time-consuming. It should be remembered however that this is the price these men and women pay for the satisfaction of owning and directing the economic world in which they live.

Partly their satisfaction is one of savings on a modest scale. But in no small part it is a deep psychological satisfaction. It is a sense of participation in the decisions that shape the lives of all. It is "we" rather than "they" who determine the nature of the economic life in which all must exist.

As in any movement so extensive there is naturally a wide range of opinion as to ultimate objectives. For some co-operators the aim is a socialized society controlled by democratic vote. For others the movement is a brake or check on the trend toward socialization or state capitalism. This, as Mr. Greer points out, is the strong line taken by the International Co-operative Alliance in a resolution demanding "freedom of activity on the basis of its own principles." This significant resolution said: "That the co-operative movement wherever a regulated economy in some form or other has been put in power rejects measures that hinder the national or international development of its activity, just as it rejects any effort in a socialistic economic state to concentrate the whole economic activity in the hands of public bodies."

In other words co-operation provides an element of competition in a free society. This is a healthy attitude in a society where industries have been dominated by cartel arrangements and monopolies as in Great Britain. It was comparatively easy for government to nationalize what was already a monopoly and in many instances, such as the coal mines, a moribund and slothful monopoly. British co-operation has often been arbitrary and doctrinaire. But, as the author shows, it has also had room for development and growth in a variety of ways. The experience of one country cannot be superimposed upon another country. But this book contains a great deal about the meaning of democracy, economic democracy as well as political democracy, from which Americans can learn.

# ACKNOWLEDGMENT

*footnote*

"CONSUMPTION is the sole end and purpose of all production. . . ." Thus wrote Adam Smith in *An Inquiry into the Nature and Causes of the Wealth of Nations*. My book is an outgrowth of the conviction that our producer-minded society is overlooking this fundamental truth—to its peril.

Consumer co-operation, which has been called brotherhood economics, is taking on new importance, not only as an instrument of mass distribution, but as a social device. Asking no favors from any government, and holding that production is for man, not man for production, the consumer movement as developed in Great Britain has become a major bulwark against the onset of the omnipotent state.

While new forms of absolutism compete for the minds of men only the group loyalties that fortify the individual and underlie society are capable of meeting the emergency. Men without such ties, formal or informal, may easily fall into the feeling that as individuals they are too insignificant or powerless to cope with the circumstances of our times.

As frustrations mount, the search becomes more important for ways to widen the participation of men and women in the solution of problems that are as much ethical as economic. It is well to keep in mind the third right of the Declaration of Independence, the very sum and purpose of Life and Liberty. That pursuit of Happiness, which by a fortunate turn escaped being termed the pursuit of Property, is not conducted in solitary fashion but through association, friendly, warm, responsive, giving and receiving in turn. Only thus is assured the fullest enjoyment of life's possibilities, and not by divorcing means from ends.

The path of my pilgrimage to England and Scotland in the latter half of 1953 was smoothed by letters of introduction to men and women outstanding in the British movement. My thanks for these to Murray D. Lincoln, president of the Co-operative League of the United States of America; Howard A. Cowden, founder of the Consumers Co-operative Association; Glenn W. Thompson, public relations director of Midland Co-operatives; John K. Friesen, now extension director of the University of British Columbia, formerly of the Manitoba Pool Elevators; and to the Rev. Leo R. Ward of the University of Notre Dame, himself the author of two books on co-operation.

Thanks overseas to Robert Southern, general secretary, Desmond Flanagan, librarian, and A. L. Sugar, publicity officer, all of the Co-operative Union; W. P. Watkins and Miss Gertrude F. Polley, of the International Co-operative Alliance; Dr. Margaret Digby of the Horace Plunkett Foundation; H. W. Shopland, P. R. Barnes and Arthur Moore, of London Co-operative Society; F. J. Comerton and William J. Morton, Royal Arsenal Co-operative Society; J. H. Halliwell, public relations officer, South Suburban Society; F. Savin, president of Rochdale Equitable Pioneers; F. Tootil of the *Co-operative News*, and William Ingham, information officer of the Co-operative Wholesale Society.

My stay in Scotland was marked by the great hospitality of Neil S. Beaton, former president of the Scottish Co-operative Wholesale Society, and J. Douglas, assistant secretary; William Grant, general manager of the flour and allied departments, and Andrew McBride, dairy and farm manager, for the same agency. Particularly helpful in Edinburgh were David Shaw, secretary of St. Cuthbert's, and J. N. White, manager of the dry goods department.

The list is inexhaustible. All conclusions drawn from my stay in Britain are my own, and are not to be ascribed to any of my contacts.

PAUL GREER

# CO-OPERATIVES
## THE BRITISH ACHIEVEMENT

## [ I ]

# LIFE DEMANDS A SOLUTION

### 1. The Perils of Indifference

OF THE many approaches to happier and fuller lives, the shortest way once seemed political. Events of a later day have discovered many pitfalls dug by the complicated machinery of the state. Power madness, the passion to enforce conformity, the acceptance of any means however unworthy and corrupting to a desirable end—these are crimes against the integrity and freedom of the individual.

Nothing could be more mistaken than to believe that society is crystallized into its final and unchangeable form, or that any possible change must go in the direction of further centralization. But if a better form of society is to be developed, this will be an association of equals, one in which initiative is reawakened and encouraged, with higher ideals and deeper principles.

Such a new environment can evolve simply and naturally once a sense of direction replaces the aimless drift of expediency and circumstance. Fundamental to a change at once efficient and ethical is the general acceptance of the consumer interest as paramount. When the producer function is recognized as a means, and not an end, new and fairer objectives come into view.

Through voluntary co-operation such unity of purpose becomes possible—even in the commercial sequence of producer-distributor-consumer.

Already sizable groups have organized for consumer education

1

as a means of minimizing exploitation of the public by the makers and sellers of the various items that go to compose a living standard. Simultaneously mergers and combinations are occurring on an unprecedented scale, threatening eventually to deprive the consumer of any choice in the market place.

Co-operation can establish automatic safeguards against the economic practices that result in alternation of periods of boom and bust.

Consumer education is important as a first step. It must break the spell of mass hypnosis by which the slogans and repetitions of advertising lure high-pressure sales. But something more than strong-willed resistance is required if the consumer is to remain immune to the mesmerism of the Svengalis of profit making.

Educating the consumer, if it succeeds, will make a co-operator out of *her*.

And the consumer is a *her*, for except in the most wealthy circles 70 to 80 per cent of all family income goes through the wives' hands. One definition of a consumer could be simply *a housewife*.

A beautiful and a hopeful quality of modern life is that self-interest has extended its range to include social feeling. Self-preservation is seen to be something more than an individual problem. The welfare of each person depends on the higher development of humanity as a whole.

Not competition or collusion, but co-operation, releases the creative power that animates each man and woman. This cohesive influence extends to the national and international planes, signaling the possibilities of peaceful understanding in which rivalries are replaced by mutual aid. Self-interest which once seemed a narrow lane leading to individual advantage has become a broad highway for the progress of humanity on the long haul.

There are no shortcuts to social advancement, and without the animating spirit no mechanized device, no improvisation of physical science can result in social progress.

This book, describing objectively the benefits of more than a century of consumer co-operation in Great Britain, shows the possibilities of unifying the yearnings of the spirit with the process of day-to-day living.

As surely as the Lord helps those who help themselves, co-operators are doubly blessed, since they also help each other. Accompanying monetary advantages are many social gains, including a rise in the standard of living and the inner satisfactions of finding effective outlets for joint endeavor.

Through more than one hundred years of success, the consumer movement has given the working people of Britain the conviction that they can do big things. Still retaining their spirit of individual freedom, they have learned to think and act collectively. From shopkeeping the co-operatives have expanded into manufacturing, insurance and banking. And along the way men and women members have gained political confidence.

British consumer co-operation is important to Americans as an inspiring rehearsal of possibilities here, as well as in less developed areas of the world. In its simplest terms, this is self-service through voluntary group effort. As a form of voluntary social action, the Rochdale techniques may be the rival, an agent or a supplement to an increasingly collective state.

In Britain today one shop out of every thirty is a co-op. More than one-eighth of the retail trade of the country goes over these counters. Co-op dairies supply one in three families with milk. Every fifth family depends on a co-op bakery for its bread. With a membership of more than 11,000,000 men and women these stores provide one-fifth of all households with their tea and their coal. Finally, one-fourth of all funerals are conducted co-operatively.

The pattern that has proved so successful traces back 111 years to the Equitable Pioneers of Rochdale, a Lancashire mill town in the foothills north of Manchester. True, co-operative purchasing developed elsewhere at an earlier date. Scotland claims the oldest surviving group, dating back to 1812 at Lennoxtown. The Fenwick Weavers Society in 1769 was supplying its members with the necessaries of life, but it disappeared, as did a London agency set up in 1821.

Great achievements have come from the thrifty pooling of meager resources and the massing of household buying power. The family that invests in a co-op share has cast its votes for a form of enterprise that spreads ownership, fights exploitation, spurs efficiency and builds community spirit. The sense of participation in the major process of supplying vital human needs has developed a population responsible and interested in having a definite stake in their country.

A soul-satisfying sense of unity emanates from group activity involving good will, mutual respect and common ends. The hope of the future lies in the realization that there can be a role for each to play, that no life need be without significance.

In England today the Co-operative Wholesale Society, established and maintained by one thousand retail co-ops, is the largest flour miller, soap and margarine manufacturer outside the combines. It employs more than 50,000 workers with annual wages exceeding $49,000,000. As great as any other such enterprise in the world, its far-flung interests include some two hundred mills, factories, farms and other productive undertakings. In partnership with its Scottish opposite number, it owns extensive tea plantations in Ceylon and India, and operates three tea factories, a coffee factory and a cocoa and chocolate works. These two wholesale agencies, the English and the Scottish, have joined with the great Swedish Kooperativa Förbundet in a plant making electric lamps. Among other products of the Scottish movement are tweed, linoleum, shoes, clothing of all kinds, cigarettes, furniture, paper and even soft drinks.

Meanwhile consumer co-operation is making headway in the United States and Canada. Though we can learn much from British experience it would be a mistake to attempt to duplicate the exact pattern from country to country. In spreading from one land to another co-operation changes in form and motivation. The source of co-operation in the England of the 1840s lay in the hardships of early industrialization, wage deficiencies and a poor system of distribution. Later development in Sweden resulted from the impositions of monopolies and the need for a competitive yardstick.

In the United States periodic industrial and financial lapses lend point to the danger inherent in a producer-oriented economy. A reorganization of effort demands a system of distribution designed primarily to meet human needs, not solely for profit. As the consumer, long exploited by his own ignorance, begins to inform himself, he realizes that present-day selling methods widen margins and encourage industrial waste. Depressions have shown that mass production loses its efficiency if there is failure of mass distribution. Wasteful marketing methods, excessive margins and costly efforts to divert demand to more profitable channels of supply seem periodically to deplete the purchasing power of consumers.

Where a monopoly or oligopoly finds it profitable to restrict production in pursuit of higher prices, co-operation has its incentive as a method of plenty.

A co-op also keeps the proceeds of trade in the home community. The semi-annual refund of co-operative savings produces the busiest period for storekeepers of all sorts and affiliations. This return of what amounts to an overcharge of customers (what ordinarily goes to business proprietors as profit) is usually spent promptly for deferred family needs. In the single city of Derby the co-op pays back $500,000 twice a year to its members and patrons. The wide-spreading branches of the London Co-operative Society burgeon with more than $5,000,000 a year as a dividend on purchases and interest on share capital. The more goods a member has bought, the larger his share of the patronage refund. If he decides not to withdraw his savings, their amount is automatically credited to his account, earning 2.5 per cent interest.

The positive values of consumer co-operation in Great Britain —and they are not solely pecuniary—have profound meaning for Americans, particularly for those wives and mothers who have grown skeptical of the blandishments of chromium-plated profit enterprise. What family shoppers want to know is where they can get the most for their money or the best quality for a given price.

Various psychological attitudes also are involved. In simpler days the customer received special attention that gave him or her a feeling of importance. Every sale was a matter of importance also to the proprietor. In the impersonal relationship of the present a customer feels like a midget and the individual has no other function than as a statistic. No store wants to lose his trade, but only because his defection might indicate a trend due to some faulty sales appeal.

Perhaps the greatest possibilities of co-operative growth in the United States are to be found among people with an instinctive horror of suffocating under the blanketing of big business. Particularly among farmers this proud spirit of free association survives, no more smothered here than in Britain.

The actual and the potential strength of the spirit of co-operation has appeared to be clearer to its opposition than to many of its practitioners. A staff correspondent of the *Wall Street Journal* made first-page news more than ten years ago of the formation of an American business pressure group to lobby for restrictions on the spread of co-ops.

"They are selling foodstuffs to city dwellers; buying machinery, fertilizer and seed for farmers," a Washington dispatch to the *Wall Street Journal* said. "They are selling insurance and extending credit. They are making cheese, refining oil and finishing lumber. Altogether they deal in a great variety of enterprise, from delivering babies to performing burial rites. . . ."

What these adversaries knew was that in Britain self-help and mutual aid had built the co-ops into the nation's largest enterprise. First steps had been taken to make improved human relations the dominant motive in economic process. In America, as in Britain, business-as-usual decided that what could not be defeated by economic competition should be wrecked through political machination.

A Congressional "Small Business Committee" by 1947 was holding hearings on co-operatives under the guidance of a chairman and a counsel whose open hostility, particularly to such consumer enterprises as at Greenbelt, near Washington, defeated the obvious purpose of their inquiry.

Continually small businessmen have been used as a screen in the gigantic political effort of great aggregations of industrial and financial capital to limit free enterprise as exemplified in the co-operative movement. Standards of production and distribution have been set largely by the motive of profit, in which the happiness of the workers is incidental, prosperity accidental and the consumer exploitable.

In Britain, too, a certain amount of hostility to co-ops has been whipped up by trader interests and sections of the press. The Beaverbrook publications have joined the attack, purportedly in behalf of small merchants. These journalistic guns, however, are never trained on any of the great combines that are masticating one small business after another. In most advanced industrial societies the little merchant is in a precarious marginal position, but not because of the co-ops.

What modern man has to learn is that it is through the group that social progress comes. The important thing at this turning point in the history of mankind is to understand the significance of people working together in a spirit of warm confidence. Voluntary co-operation makes men economically free, and no pressure groups should be permitted to bar the way.

## 2. Frontiers of the New Day

As a decentralizing influence the co-operative idea is entering a planetary contest of principles with giant government. Politically this organizing of the consumer interest stands out against the encroachments of the omni-competent state.

Substitution of the service motive instead of profit gives some resemblance between co-operative enterprise and government-owned operation. Yet co-operation, seeking only a fair field and no favors, contrasts simply with the elements of monopoly in state enterprise. Many organized consumers hold fast to the position that co-operation itself is a form of social ownership. With

members in about half of all British households, the point is made
that co-operation offers a non-paternalistic alternative to across-
the-board nationalization. Thus the taint of regimentation would
be removed, and any minority left free to pursue its own competitive and private path.

"Co-operators do not associate for trade alone; we believe co-
operation is a moral way of life which supersedes wasteful
competition," reads a handbook prepared for the 45,000 members
at Cambridge. "Co-operators have believed from the first that by
supporting their own society they are helping to build a better
world."

Truly, the frontiers of this new day lie in the relationships of
the individual to business and industry, and to the state. Much of
our pioneering henceforth is to be in the educational wilderness
—and the spirit of adventure will find its opportunity in brave
thinking by daring minds.

A clearer distinction between a producer-motivated economy
and one that is consumer-minded is urgently needed.

To Americans who may not recognize the ultimate importance
of the consumer function, co-operation is often known only as a
method of marketing farm production. Or if they have looked
about to observe urban developments it may appear as nothing
more than an odd way of obtaining groceries. The democratic
implications are apt to pass unseen. The pooling of purchasing
power, the local control of such enterprises from the bottom up
instead of the top down, the tendency to lower retail prices and
to fit supply to known demand—these give new economic dignity to the common man.

If democracy is rule by the people, it is possible to have it
politically and to lack it economically. What is now happening
over the world is that those who have been the puppets of economic happenstance have begun to realize their power to plan
their own future—and that of their nations.

Up to the time of the First World War the British co-ops had
been politically neutral, depending on lobbying through their
Parliamentary Committee. As the war proceeded, many co-ops

found themselves unable to obtain their share of scarce or rationed goods. There developed also a suspicion that the conscription machinery was too much under the influence of local merchants. At all events the call-up stripped the societies of clerks, crippling operations. Finally, destructive taxes were proposed in the House of Commons, moving the Parliamentary Committee to request the Prime Minister to receive a co-op delegation.

Though Lloyd George was too busy to see the co-operators he still found time to welcome petitioners from the Jockey Club. This was the straw that broke the back of political neutrality. The next Co-operative Congress worked out a plan for unity of action with the trade unions and decided to seek representation in Parliament.

Far different was the consideration accorded the co-operative movement during the Second World War—consulted in every detail of food supply and rationing, recognized as a mainstay of democratic morale.

Formation of the Co-operative party in 1919 was financed by fees from affiliated societies. Something more than half of the retail associations, comprising about 85 per cent of the total membership, now subscribes to the Central Political Fund. The party is responsible to the Co-operative Union, the advisory and co-ordinating agency established at Manchester in 1869. It works with the Labour party both in Parliament and on local authorities. The trade unions, the Labour party and the co-operative movement have a further link in the National Council of Labour, which includes eight representatives from each organization.

Membership in the British co-operative movement, however, is distributed throughout the working and middle classes. It embraces true-blue Tories, red-hot Socialists and millions without any extreme coloration. The president of the Leeds society, which has 150,000 members, is a prominent Conservative political figure. A number of smaller co-ops, mainly in non-industrial areas, have refused to authorize the halfpence-per-member deduction to finance the Co-operative party. Most recently the Plymouth society, whose executive chief was the president of the 1954 Co-operative Congress, has voted again to abstain from party affiliation.

This decision may reflect a growing reluctance to accept the theories of all-out nationalization. Experience has taught the Co-operative party, with its eighteen members of Parliament, that the form of public ownership set up by the 1945 Labour government is not perfect.

The management of such great undertakings as the coal mines and the railroads has been placed in the hands of highly paid boards out of touch with consumers as well as with the workers. The change of bosses still retains many of those who represented the previous owners. A lack of enthusiasm among the workers and the growth of bureaucracy leave a discontented and unconvinced consuming public.

Some years ago Leonard S. Woolf wrote of the co-ops as the business wing of the modern state. In his book, *Co-operation and the Future of Industry*, he reasoned that the actual power of citizens to control a municipalized milk supply would be less than if the dairy business were in the hands of a co-operative.

"The municipality has no organs like the quarterly meeting and the management committee, which put the consumer in direct relation with his representatives and the salaried staff who are immediately responsible for managing the business," Mr. Woolf said.

A debate among readers of the *Co-operative News* indicates the spirit of independent thought and free speech characteristic of the movement. Denying that the Rochdale Pioneers were thinking solely of their own pockets, one correspondent wrote that they were concerned with the distribution of power, which they did not want to seize but only to gain slowly, equally and collectively for all men. He went on to deny that co-operation and socialism have nothing in common, though he conceded that each uses different means in the drive for full democracy.

In rejoinder a co-operator writing from South Africa stated that the original belief was that all men would learn to co-operate because it was in each man's interest to do so. "Consequently, they believed that co-operation would expand indefinitely until it embraced the whole of human life and at no point would compulsion be necessary," the argument ran.

As long as faith in the ability to expand indefinitely continued, according to this interpretation, the members in general were not interested in political action and were hostile to state socialism. "The belief that co-operation would expand indefinitely evaporated in the years before 1914 and because of this, co-operators turned to political action to further their cause," it concluded.

Any rise in the general welfare depends on the higher development of humanity. The wider range of social feeling today conceives of man existing and developing as part of a greater purpose, including both unity and variety, freedom and responsibility. The imminence of total destruction has given a more earnest hearing for religious idealism and the philosophy of a better world.

Co-operation and recognition of the full importance of the consumer function are steps along the way. Not alone for their physical results, but for the effect on the minds and hearts of men. It is possible to think of things worse even than atomic warfare—psychological attacks in which men are manipulated, their standards destroyed and their personalities maimed by the myth of a master class or a super race or a single leader.

The doctrine of every man for himself mistakenly disguises underconsumption as overproduction. The accumulation of grain and dairy surpluses in the United States while many areas around the world go hungry is viewed generally as a burden rather than as an opportunity. Statistical studies indicate that this surplus of milk would not have existed if each American had taken one good swallow more—one-twentieth of a pint per day. One extra pat of butter a day for two out of five persons would have left no accumulation.

A Nebraska co-operative editor, L. S. Herron, says that if all the families in the United States had the necessary purchasing power for a liberal diet, our people would consume all we produce, with the possible exception of wheat, which always has been raised to feed the hungry overseas.

Some years ago a great Japanese advocate of co-operation, on a speaking tour of America, was asked why there had been so little development in our cities.

"Americans have not suffered enough," was his reply.

A businessman of my acquaintance was quick to comment that we should feel blessed that co-operation was not forced by hardships. My own reaction is otherwise: one of uneasiness if only adversity can be counted on to stimulate the sense of community of interest.

### 3. Rainbow Flag of Promise

Not despair, but rather high hope for the future inspires the spread of co-operation. In thirty-three different countries, on all five continents, organizations with a total membership of 114,-000,000 persons are affiliated with the International Co-operative Alliance, of which Sir Harry Gill is president. It promotes, through auxiliary trading, petroleum, banking and insurance organizations, direct relations between co-ops of all kinds and in all lands. The United Nations has given it the right to participate in the work of the Economic and Social Council.

The ICA is a clarifying as well as a unifying influence, and its monthly publication, the *Review of International Co-operation*, has English, French and German editions. After eight years of committee study, the ICA Congress has singled out four essential attributes of what is known around the world as Rochdale co-operation. The question arose at the conference in Vienna, back in 1930, and it was 1937 before the answer was boiled down to this:

1. Open membership
2. Democratic control
3. Distribution of surplus in proportion to purchases
4. Limited interest on capital.

Three of the original characteristics of the Equitable Pioneers, well to be respected but not an acid test of true co-operation, were defined as political and religious neutrality, cash trading, and the promotion of education.

The original Rochdale "principles" were adaptable as methods fitted to their times and needs. Consumers then were up against extortionate small traders who were not above adulterating and short-weighting food supplies, which constituted the bulk of household purchases. Different tactics now are required. For one thing, groceries, long the mainstay of co-op business, require a smaller part of the workers' income and demand has risen for items once considered beyond their means. Some of these could not be obtained on the ready-money system.

Payment for bread and for milk delivered to the door is more conveniently made at the end of the week. Substantial trade has developed throughout Britain on the hire purchase or installment plan, as well as in what are known as "mutuality clubs," with small weekly collections.

Belgium, for one, has shown the feasibilty of separate Catholic and Socialist co-op networks, dispensing with religious and political neutrality.

The Swedish delegates unsuccessfully advanced the principles of cash trading and political neutrality in the ICA discussions. They were more successful in obtaining agreement that the early Rochdale practice of selling at market prices need not be followed by strong modern co-ops. The Pioneers, it was pointed out, had accepted current price levels as a simple way of assuring a margin between income and outgo; a further consideration was to avoid price wars by too evident undercutting.

Scandinavian consumers have tamed one monopoly after another by an aggressive pricing policy. Not only members, but the public generally have enjoyed the immediate benefits of lower living costs without the necessity of waiting for a semi-annual patronage refund. In Sweden the general price level has been held down even for non-members who shop outside the co-ops.

In one ICA debate it was agreed also that any resort to high co-op prices for the sake of swelling dividends would encourage

a general increase in living costs. The true function of co-operation was defined as checking exploitation of the needs of consumers.

In many instances the co-ops tend to set current prices for the
profit sector of trade. It is only co-operation that stands between
the consumer and cartel agreements abolishing competition in
behalf of price maintenance.

As of now, the avowed purpose of consumer co-operation is
to protect and increase spending power, on the theory that earning the paycheck is only half the problem. The consumer is becoming more insistent on his right to be considered. In the meantime ownership is widened, group experience is developed and
average men and women become acquainted with the facts of
business life and governmental restrictions and burdens.

Under the co-op requirements of open membership and
democratic control, membership is without discrimination of race,
religion or political affiliation. Each member has only one vote,
regardless of the number of shares held.

Just as it is the man, not the money, that votes in membership
meetings, so is money made the servant instead of the master.
Interest on an investment in co-op shares is paid at a fixed rate,
usually nominal or low—no matter how large the earnings or
surplus may be. The savings are refunded to members in proportion to the amount of their purchases.

Each year Co-operative Day is celebrated in countries having
ICA membership. A pageant presented by London's South
Suburban Society included greetings from co-operative groups
in many nations and a reading of the ICA manifesto for support
of the essentials of world peace, which were thus outlined at its
Copenhagen Congress:

That in every country the people shall enjoy the fullest measure
of self-expression, self-government, freedom of association, freedom
of movement within their own frontiers and beyond them;
That standards of living in under-developed countries shall be
raised so that the gross inequalities between them and the more advanced countries disappear;

That the endeavour of the United Nations Organization to improve the health, security and welfare of mankind shall be loyally supported by its member countries;

That the production of war materials of every kind in every country shall be brought and kept under effective international control.

The rainbow flag, with its many colors indicating the harmony of diversity, was flown as the emblem of the Alliance, and the celebration closed with the singing of T. W. Mercer's song of the flag:

> Proclaim a common people's peace,
> Justice for all mankind . . .

The world-wide scope of co-operation also is stressed by the International Labor Office in publications issued from Geneva, Switzerland. In a single number of their reports information is given about workers' co-operative housing in Turkey, Greek urban co-ops, Quebec's co-operative council, co-op land settlement in Israel, credit unions in Canada, France's 35th National Congress of the Federation of Agricultural Co-operative, Mutual Aid and Credit Societies and the Women's Guild in the German Federal Republic.

The United States is represented by three articles, one on a co-op management development program, another on the co-operative organization of artificial insemination of cattle in Puerto Rico and a short account of developments in Alaska.

From this we learn that after a small beginning by a branch of the Bureau of Indian Affairs in 1939, the government-sponsored Alaska Native Industries Co-operative Association, "whose president is an Eskimo, has developed until it now has fifty-two member societies to be found along the Bering Sea and Arctic Ocean coasts, and inland along the banks of the Yukon, Kuskowim and Tanana rivers."

There is also a society on Little Diomede Island, near the Russian outposts. The native stores are not subsidized by the United

States government, the ILO states, but some of them have obtained credits for local development.

One Eskimo co-op store has built a sawmill and another has set up a village lighting plant. Among the best selling lines in the stores are tins of tallow in two grades, one for human consumption and the other for sled dogs. This Co-operative Association has an office in Seattle, Washington, which looks after purchase of goods for the North and also acts as an outlet for Eskimo products, including hand-worked ivory, fur pelts and seal and whale oils for paint and drug manufacturers.

Hardly any American, whatever his devotion to profit enterprise, will find objection to official encouragement of such collective action in the snowy waste, where giant corporations could scarcely hope to sell refrigerators, or automobiles or ready-mix pancakes.

# [ II ]

# ROADS FROM ROCHDALE

## 1. A New Look at Toad Lane

So long as the tradition of Rochdale survives men will not lose the capacity for active participation in the making of significant decisions. People's values may change but the right to decide critical issues is at the base of co-operative democracy and not to be given up. Hitler's seizure of the German co-operatives showed the dictator's fear of the alert social feeling inherent in such organic groups. Nor was it an accident that made a co-operative brewery the center of Danish underground resistance to the Nazis.

Political structures, like partisan powers, are transitory. Economic geography has its peaks and valleys. But the riches of the human spirit, the confidence in one another that marks democratic living, these multiply with the growth of a sense of individual responsibility. At the everyday level the co-operative way restores and safeguards the dignity of man as a decision maker.

In a congratulatory message on the one hundredth anniversary of the founding of the Rochdale Equitable Pioneers' Society, President Franklin D. Roosevelt sent these words from the United States: "The weavers of Rochdale, who founded the modern co-operative enterprise, balanced independence with interdependence; self-interest with good will; and action with foresight."

These Pioneers were younger than they appear with their bearded faces in the old pictures. Three of the number were only nineteen years old, and several others were only in their twenties or thirties. With the sum of £28 accumulated from threepenny contributions they opened a little co-op shop in narrow, hilly Toad Lane back in 1844.

Abraham Greenwood, who progressed from Rochdale to Manchester to become the first president of the Co-operative Wholesale Society, gave this interpretation of the overall purpose:

As co-operators we have to teach mankind, that as humanity is one sole body, all we, being members of that body, are bound to labour for its development, and to seek to render life more harmonious, vigorous and active. . . . Ask yourself as to every act you perform within the circle of family or country, if what I now do were done by and for all men, would it be beneficial or injurious to humanity; and if your conscience tells you it would be injurious, desist—desist even though it seems that an immediate advantage to your country or your family would be the result.

A fortunate provision of the bylaws by which each member held only one vote irrespective of his number of shares shielded this early venture from investor control. A bank failure at Rochdale brought a flood of thrifty investment in the comparative safety of co-operative shares. This supplied capital for building a large store on the site of a tabernacle where John Wesley had preached. Even now this is sacred ground to the millions of persons the world over who participate in the feeling of personal growth and ownership of a stake in the community through the practical application in their own lives of the lessons of Rochdale.

Both history and literature tell of the hardships accompanying the industrial revolution. Disturbances over the introduction of power looms resulted in ten deaths at Rochdale in 1828. The hunger, debt, unemployment and hopeless misery appear most clearly in Carlyle's *Past and Present* and in a group of novels including two by Disraeli, *Endymion* and *Sybil*. Never to be forgotten are the descriptions of the truck shops, those debt traps from which workers drew supplies from company stores or lost their jobs.

Charles Kingsley, who had a share in the encouragement of co-operation, pictured the background of the times in *Yeast* and *Alton Locke*. Mrs. Elizabeth Gaskell, best known for her sentimental novel, *Cranford*, laid the foundation of her literary career with *Mary Barton: A Tale of Manchester Life*, a realistic account of the ferment of Chartist days. Charles Dickens was later to sum up the scene in *Hard Times*, giving the name of Coketown to the area of Manchester and Rochdale.

Lord Byron knew Rochdale in a lighthearted way, where his family estates centered, but not with the depth of interest felt by Mrs. Gaskell as the wife of a Manchester minister. Lady Byron, who divorced the poet, contributed generously for the spread of co-operation through Dr. William King of Brighton, one of its first advocates.

In the days when tax-supported schools were unknown, John Bright praised the educational classes set up by the Pioneers out of their savings. Richard Cobden, famous advocate of free trade, represented Rochdale in Parliament, but it took Gracie Fields, who was born in that town, to popularize in song, "The Co-op Shop."

There are now 30,000 members at Rochdale, with a capital investment of $1,500,000 and a yearly trade more than double that amount. Each member must hold at least two shares, valued at £1 each, to which dividends from purchases will be credited. When payment is not made in full, the rules require installments on a share amounting to about 46 cents every three months. Eligibility to management committees requires ownership of ten fully paid-up shares. Further official qualifications require purchase of goods to the amount of £25 in a year if single and of £50 if married. Members may withdraw their shares in cash at par value on due notice.

To a certain extent the co-op refund, or "divi," is regarded as a sort of savings bank account. A Co-operative Wholesale department manager recalls that his mother left her divi to accumulate year after year until it was finally withdrawn as his wedding present. On their sixtieth anniversary as members of a co-op at Huddersfield an aged couple counted $1,000 in patronage refunds. At Gloucester, Reuben E. Chappell deposited 3 pence on a co-op share in 1887; after forty years accrued dividends on purchases and interest on shares exceeded $1,400. In fifty-three years, by 1940, his total in shares and loan capital had grown to $3,480.

Rochdale's half yearly refund is 8 pence on each pound of purchases, about 3.75 per cent, in contrast to the 10 per cent paid before the war. Controlled margins under rationing and inability to pay a dividend on that part of prices represented by high taxes have resulted in a downward trend for refunds in almost all localities.

The retail trade of the co-operative movement, now well above $2,000,000,000 a year, returns savings of more than $116,000,000. The country-wide average is a shilling on each pound spent for goods, or 5 per cent. A rate of 2 shillings is reported by the 4,600-member society at Windy Nook, and of 2 shillings 7 pence, better than 12 per cent, by Murton society, membership 4,000, in County Durham.

This is what remains after substantial provision for employee pensions, taxation, allocations to reserves, depreciation, educational, political and charitable grants, bonuses to employees and group life insurance premiums, the cost of which has to be borne out of net surplus before the refund is calculated.

Just as women had a vote in co-operatives long before it was given them politically, so also were their property rights put ahead of the law. Although a woman's property legally was held to become her husband's on marriage, husbands who attempted to withdraw their wives' co-op holdings usually were defeated in their aims. Accumulating patronage dividends tempted many a man, but delay in acting on demands allowed the cashier to notify the wives, who were able to act first.

The total British experiences have significance for Americans by illustrating the function of small savings as capital funds for expansion of co-op services. In Rochdale, dividends that are not collected are added to capital, bearing interest at 3 per cent. Loan capital is accepted in multiples of £5 at 2.5 per cent interest, subject to one month's notice of withdrawal. Small savings also may be banked, up to £2 a week to a maximum of £50, at 3.33 per cent. As a further benefit, each member comes under a collective life insurance plan with a premium rate of 1½ pence in each pound's purchase. This is paid by the society on behalf of all, and covers spouses as well. The maximum benefit, based on volume of purchasing, is £40.

The fullest information concerning services is provided for new members in a letter of welcome provided by W. S. Greenwood, the general secretary, who thus enumerates the opportunities for self-service:

Wherever you live in Rochdale there is one of our 53 Grocery branches near your home. Look down the list attached and choose a convenient shop—they are all eager to serve you. And note also the Butchery, Pork, Confectionery, Drapery and Outfitting branches. The Central Departments comprising—Tailoring, Drapery, Outfitting, Furnishing, Radio, Pharmacy and Tudor Café are at your service with a variety of goods at competitive prices, plus dividend.

Shoes for repair may be left at any Grocery branch, to which they will be returned in a few days.

Coal registrations are welcomed and orders for Coke, Ovoids, Briquettes and Logs may be placed at the shops by registered customers.

Bread and Confectionery are delivered by electric van.

The Co-operative Dairies deliver daily the finest pasteurised and T.T. Milk.

The Co-operative Laundries collect and return at regular times.

Our Funeral Furnishing Department gives a sympathetic and efficient service; again instructions may be left at any Grocery branch.

An Optical service is provided at 13 Oldham Road, and your National Insurance prescriptions will be carefully dispensed at the Pharmacy, 13 Yorkshire Street.

You can invest up to £500 in your share account and other members of your family can also join and have separate accounts.

To illustrate the changes that have developed through the years, the president of Rochdale society, F. Savin, takes a time-blackened key and leads the way from the large headquarters building to the original shop at No. 31 Toad Lane. Inside the narrow building with its bow windows and its bull's-eye glass is a museum maintained by the Co-operative Union with funds subscribed from many parts of the world. The old iron scales, designed to give full measure—an innovation in the days of the tommy shops, stand on a wooden counter. Close by is a replica of the twenty-eight pounds of butter, the sugar, flour and oatmeal of the original stock. Tied to a hook by the window are the traditional twenty-four tallow candles.

Mr. Savin points out the wrought-iron gas fixture hanging from a huge beam, and tells of a gas company manager in the hungry forties of the last century who refused to supply lighting service to what he considered likely to be a short-lived venture.

The back room of the museum is filled with photographs, and cases containing old account books, pamphlets and early manuscripts of bylaws and other Pioneer proceedings. Yes, conditions have changed, the president of this 111-year-old association agrees. Co-operatives, originally on the cash-and-carry principle, no longer regard credit as an unmitigated evil, and as for delivering purchases, the co-op today operates fifty motor vehicles.

A rule adopted in 1854 states: "The officers of this society shall not, in any case, nor any pretense, either sell or purchase any article except for ready money. Any officer acting contrary to this law shall be fined 10s., and be disqualified from performing the duties of such office."

But almost directly across Toad Lane from the first shop are the modern furniture showrooms where co-operatively produced television and radio sets as well as all manner of household furnishings may be bought on credit terms.

In the same spirit of realism the original formula of political neutrality has gone by the boards. By vote of the membership the Pioneers now are enrolled as a unit of the Co-operative party. In an expansive moment Mr. Savin gives it as his opinion that the limit of nationalization has not yet been reached. He considers that land should be under complete control by the state, and he would not stop short until "the great combines and monopolies have been extirpated, and the sordid effects of capitalism nullified."

As a workman Mr. Savin supports his family on the wages of a loom overlooker in a Rochdale textile mill. His fees as president of the co-op amount to $87 a year. The eight committeemen receive $73 for meeting once a week throughout the year —and for special sessions an extra 5 shillings (70 cents). Some feeling is developing, what with wage rises for clerks and other employees under trade union contracts, for more generous recognition of board members. At Rochdale they include two employees of the co-op elected by the membership meeting, a clerk, an engineer, a retired railwayman, a wool worker, a carpenter and a commercial traveler.

"Service is an honor and has many compensations apart from monetary reward," President Savin commented. "You've got to believe in the movement for what you put into it, not for what you get out of it."

## 2. MUTUAL AID IN ACTION

If shore leave for American sailors reaching Portsmouth includes a dance, it is likely to be in the spacious public ballroom operated nightly by the local co-operative. Downstairs is a restaurant under the same auspices. Possibly the connection with the co-operative goes unnoticed, not only here but in a chain of drugstores and a chorus of specialty shops. But if any of the visitors drops into a department store it may well be at Co-operative House, an extensive new building replacing the headquarters bombed out in the late war.

American co-operative leaders and more recently a group of co-op managers from Sweden have made this a port of call as one of the most advanced British developments. There are seventeen larger retail groups than this 87,000-member Portsea Island

Mutual Co-operative Society but this is one of the few with a rate of saving exceeding the prewar figure. Out of annual trade amounting to $17,000,000 there is a surplus of more than $1,000,-000 for distribution to members, 1 shilling 4 pence out of each £1 spent, better than 6.5 per cent.[1]

Portsea Mutual, now more than eighty years old, strives to meet every personal need, even from theater tickets, travel and hotel reservations to hairdressing and chimney sweeping. In addition to sixty-seven grocery and provision branches there are six mobile grocery shops, three butchery vans and a rolling dry goods store, these supplying outlying districts and new housing estates.

The naval works made Portsmouth a prime objective of war-time air raids, in which one-third of the co-op properties suffered heavily. The process of rebuilding has allowed extensive modernization. The first co-op grocery to install self-service was opened here in 1948. Since then more than a thousand others have been similarly equipped by other co-ops, a step ahead of private traders. The beginning was through the alert interest of Portsea's secretary and executive officer, J. Jacques.

"We can all learn from each other," Mr. Jacques said to me in praising American merchandising techniques. A bookcase in his office is filled with books and periodicals dealing with new developments in self-service, supermarkets and the multiples, as he calls chain stores. These publications are mainly from the United States, which he has not yet visited though he keeps abreast by his reading.

On a recent trip to Sweden he found many American innovations in use by the co-ops. Some of these, he remarked, may be carried too far, as in efforts to sell furniture and clothing by the same methods as food, the self-selection required for furniture and clothing being a different thing from the self-service for food.

[1] For purposes of easy conversion let it be said that a shilling is valued at 14 cents in United States coinage. There are 12 pence in a shilling, which gives a sixpenny piece a value of 7 cents. Since there are 20 shillings in a pound (£), this unit approximates $2.80.

Swedish co-operation, he observed, lays less stress on democracy than the English, and more on efficiency. Another impression brought back from Stockholm was that full political neutrality cannot be claimed when so many Swedish co-op leaders are active in the Social Democratic party.

One of the shortcomings of the British movement, poor attendance at membership meetings, does not exist in Sweden. As many as 25,000 persons turn out in Stockholm's 120 neighborhood districts. Entire families are admitted, even non-members. There is usually a film, a play or a concert in addition to the main business. Each member receives a small gift, such as an oven meat thermometer.

In Britain shareholders elect their own board of directors or management committee; this then hires the managers. But in Sweden the membership vote only elects a council which in turn selects and supervises the directors. These are chosen for their expert ability, whereas in Britain directors or management committeemen are consumers first and quite likely to be working in jobs having nothing to do with merchandising.

Mr. Jacques saw some advantage in Stockholm's limitation of the patronage refund to 3 per cent, with the additional surplus going to swell the reserves in good years and bad. Thus is provided more abundant and venturesome capital for expansion. In contrast, whereas some British co-operators do not withdraw their dividends, most of the savings are paid out semi-annually. And any amounts retained in the co-op treasury are eaten into by taxation.

When other means of disparaging co-operatives fail, they are charged with prospering through unwarranted tax privileges. No such accusation is true, said Mr. Jacques. Up to 1933 the British courts had held that mutual trading organizations, though they produced savings on purchases, were incapable of making profits out of the trade of their members. But now, under a new law, any undistributed surplus is taxed, though that portion refunded to members still goes free.

"In practice this tax discourages thrift, and this in institutions where thrift is fundamental," Mr. Jacques reasoned. "Suppose a society has a thousand-pound surplus at the end of the year. The question arises, shall it all be paid out so members may enjoy the whole of it, or shall we keep it in the business and give the government half of it as tax? The natural tendency to distribute the whole of it discourages reserves and expansion."

Quite different is the situation of a joint stock company. There shareholders benefit whether profits are retained or paid out. In their case any sums retained in the treasury are reflected in the rising market value of shares. But with the co-ops shares always remain at par, and shareholders are never able to cash in on earnings withheld from distribution.

Nevertheless, since its founding in 1873, Portsea Mutual has accumulated $11,000,000 in capital, including more than $2,000,-000 in loans and investments. Some of the loans are for co-operative production enterprises, others for house mortgages. Members' shares pay a fixed 3 per cent, the main distribution being in the form of the patronage refund.

The balance sheet shows an item of $80,000 for taxes and a contribution of $5,700 for the Co-operative party. Before the net surplus is computed there is also a $10,000 deduction for educational work, and allowances for death benefits, employees' welfare and old age pensioners.

As this is written both the president and vice-president of this co-op are housewives. They are members of a management commitee of nine elected by the membership. In addition to presenting quarterly reports and the annual balance sheet they appoint an executive officer and departmental managers who are responsible to the committee for the detailed conduct of business. Not more than two members who are employees can serve on the committee, and no employee can become president.

Preference in hiring goes to members and their families. Permanent employees are required to become members of the society and also to join a trade union. A personnel booklet states that wage rates negotiated with the unions are usually higher than statutory minimums. Joint consultative machinery is designed primarily to promote understanding by the exchange of views between management and staff. In each co-op district and nationally, the Co-operative Union hours and wage boards negotiate agreements.

"The society is not run for private profit but for the benefit of the members and the staff," a statement to employees reads. "The amount of the benefit the staff receive as members of the society and the extent to which the society can finance superannuation and welfare schemes, generous payment during sickness and other benefits of co-operative employment depend upon the degree of efficiency and economy in the operation of the business."

Inside the city of Portsmouth 40 per cent of the milk supply and 25 per cent of grocery rationing registrations have been in the hands of the co-op. For the entire district of six hundred square miles the co-op milk percentage is 32, groceries 22 and meat 14. It maintains its own dairy, selling well over 4,000,000 gallons a year, and a bakery producing 12,000,000 loaves of bread.

An advertisement of co-op milk and ice cream points out that the dividend amounts to one free pint in every sixteen purchased. Portsea Mutual invests in two large newspaper advertisements each week. Throughout the movement advertising is coming into increasing use though once it was felt that member loyalty would render this expenditure unnecessary.

In every railway station from Southampton to Portsmouth are large posters proclaiming the "MARK OF A THOUSAND GOOD THINGS FROM JAMS TO PRAMS—CWS." Similar reminders are carried on London busses and billboards, and the Co-operative Wholesale Society also has a huge display sign in Piccadilly.

Market research by CWS has finally discovered that mass production is made possible by spotlighting one product instead of a number of varieties of the same item. National advertising campaigns also are influencing local co-ops to observe uniform pricing of standard articles.

The great Forth bridge at Edinburgh for a long time bore the "advert," as it is called, of the Scottish Co-operative Wholesale Society. Local co-ops may compose their own slogans, as "TRADE AT THE STORE NEAREST YOUR DOOR," and at a time when rationing was modified, "PLEASED TO MEAT YOU."

No other bid for public notice has attracted half the attention, however, given a poster placed prominently in a railway station by SCWS. This read simply, "I GOT IT AT THE CO-OP."

But by sheer chance it had been pasted up beside a National Health Service billboard announcing the opening of a V.D. crusade.

### 3. SEEDS OF OLD-FASHIONED THRIFT

The co-operative refund is particularly displeasing to trade associations which are enabled by British law to fix resale prices on products that they control. Outside the co-op network there is largely a cartelized economy based on high profits and low turnover.

Operating on a non-profit basis, consumer co-ops find it necessary to provide against business contingencies and to accumulate reserves by maintaining a margin of price over expenses. This surplus when refunded in proportion to each member's patronage gives him goods or services at cost. Trade associations regard any such rebate as a delayed but still illegal method of cutting prices on restricted items.

Trade boycotts have forced the co-operatives to manufacture more and more of their own products. Thus, legalized price maintenance of many medical preparations in common use has finally been set at naught by chains of co-op drugstores which have financed their own sources of supply.

Similar restrictions by radio manufacturers threatened to shut off the supply of receiving sets on which a patronage refund was paid. Refusing to be coerced, the Co-operative Wholesale Society contracted with an electronics manufacturer for a model of its own, appropriately given the brand name "Defiant." Cabinets for this excellent low-priced line are made in one of the great co-operative furniture works. The success of this move encouraged the co-ops to become one of the first television manufacturers, again with a "Defiant" trademark.

In such ways, from its earliest days the movement has been inspired and molded by the nature of its opposition.

The three great soap plants of CWS stand today as monuments to the folly of anti-social efforts to push consumers around. Back in 1910 a number of soap makers attempted a combine through exchange of each other's shares. A sudden outcry in the popular press forced abandonment of the scheme and at the same time attracted attention to the alternative offered by the co-operative soap works. At about this time Lever Brothers, one of the large manufacturers, diminished the weight of soap bars from sixteen to fifteen ounces. Four hundred retail co-ops resolved to sell only CWS-made soap.

As the shift to co-op brands accelerated, the Lever firm filed thirty-eight suits against consumer societies, alleging it was being deprived of its business. Evidence was based on the experiences of junior employees of the company who had been sent from one co-op to another to ask specifically for Lever soap—returning only with co-op brands of somewhat similar appearance.

For two years the courts were filled with what one judge described as "an attempt by the plaintiffs to compel the defendants to stock their soaps and to abstain from selling their own soaps." On final judgment the company failed to recover damages and had to pay its own legal costs.

Scottish co-operators have been equally successful in standing off soap makers who demand that full price be charged for their products, with no semi-annual patronage refund. The threat to shut off supplies lost one company annual orders for hundreds of thousands of cakes of soap and put the Scottish Co-operative Wholesale in the business of soap manufacturing.

Within six months this consumer agency had established a sheep fat rendering plant in Australia and its own soap factory at home. Today, in spite of all efforts to prevent their expansion, the Scottish and English wholesales operate their own vegetable oil depots in West Africa, assuring adequate supplies of raw materials.

Scottish co-operators began regular importations of beef cattle from Canada as a result of a ten-year boycott by Glasgow meat dealers and auctioneers. Refusal to sell to co-op abattoirs, even in the public market, eventually was self-defeating. Particularly shocking to Highland farmers was an auctioneer's refusal of a co-op bid ten pounds higher than any other.

As part of this campaign dating from 1888, the Scottish Traders' Defense Association issued an appeal designed to sweep co-operatives from the country before they had gained full momentum. A manifesto for posting in factories and shops read as follows: "All employees who are directly or indirectly connected with any co-operative society must cease to have such connections before ———— ———— if they wish to retain their employment, or accept this intimation in lieu of the usual notice to leave."

Many Scottish employers refused any such high-handed attempt to interfere with the freedom of their workmen. And now, over sixty years later, a prosperous mixed economy includes all forms of enterprise, in which the co-ops hold an important place. SCWS employs 16,000 workers, all under trade union contracts, and the local retail members many thousands more. Through the years it has been demonstrateed that co-operation serves to check any tendency to profiteer, and its ability to enter new fields discourages exploitation in general. This massed buying power has become strong enough to influence prices, not only at retail but even on purchases from producers.

Any resultant increase in purchasing power is equivalent to raising the standard of living—a development adding employment opportunities, and good for all business. As this understanding seeps through the cracked wall of prejudice a good deal of hostile propaganda loses its effect.

There are many indications of the wider acceptance of the legitimacy of the co-operative idea. This change of attitude is evidenced by the unanimous acceptance of the great South Suburban Co-operative Society as a member of the Mottingham and Chislehurst Chamber of Commerce. The application for admission to this business association was presented by J. H. Halliwell, public relations officer of the co-op. Making it clear that this was not merely another form of trading that pays a dividend, but much more, he said: "It exists to meet the needs of its members, to devote its surpluses to educational and cultural activities as well as dividends and to extend its benefits to all who care to share them, because membership is open."

Society, he observed, is held together by voluntary co-operation, and many reforms begun by such volunteer organizations have "awakened the conscience of the nation and have become a part of our statutory system." Taking note of the strange fact that many persons outside the movement regard the Co-operative Wholesale Society as an octopus with the local co-ops as its tentacles, he showed that in reality the retail co-ops scattered up and down the country are the owners of the wholesale agency.

"Early in the history of the co-operative movement," Mr. Halliwell explained, "it was found that a great deal of trade opposition was encountered and that buyers often were boycotted. Because of this and because of the rapid growth of the movement, it was soon realized that many advantages would accrue if societies federated in order to buy more efficiently and more freely. For that purpose the Co-operative Wholesale Society and the Scottish Co-operative Wholesale Society were formed, chiefly for the wholesale handling, but they are also productive societies, as the volume of their trade easily justified their embarking in production."

Many small retail establishments in Britain as well as in the United States have come to use the co-operative pattern for their joint wholesale supply. Credit associations and even delivery systems often are operated co-operatively on a service basis, as non-profit auxiliaries.

It was against quite a different background that co-ops got their start. Only in recent years have they ventured to set up on main thoroughfares. The hostile reactions of feudalistic trading and financial interests made it desirable to attract as little attention as possible to shopping at the co-op. Light is cast on this situation by a book celebrating sixty years of the Long Eaton Society.

Out of desire to injure the cause, two bakers and a publican broke into the shop, smashing windows and damaging the sign [the account runs]. Before the magistrates, the lawyer pleaded on behalf of the culprits that it was a mere joke—a gentlemanly spree! And the magistrates, perhaps a little prejudiced against workingmen co-operators, asked the lawyers to get the matter settled out of court. This was done, the jokers paying for the damage.

In this Derbyshire town, back in 1868, a Primitive Methodist preacher, William Burns, who also managed a gas works, met secretly with four or five other non-conformists in his hayloft to plan the Long Eaton co-operative. Some forty persons attended a later organization meeting in the old Wesleyan chapel. A temporary shop was set up in a member's front room and stocked with four bags of flour, two of barley, also butter, bacon, cheese and lard.

These quarters soon proving inadequate, the goods were moved to a back-street warehouse in a handcart, the committee taking inventory on the way. By the second quarter a 3-shilling dividend was declared, amounting to 15 per cent on each £1 spent in the store. The shopman, it is related, received an increase of 2 shillings a week in his wages, "thus being allowed to share in the society's prosperity."

A great deal about human nature appears in this adventure in united action to develop a simple system to meet human needs. The pattern of association had many a brush with the tradition of individualism. In its second year, when it had grown to 166 members, the group joined the Co-operative Wholesale Society which had been set up in Manchester as a purchasing agency.

Coal deliveries, a butcher shop and the sale of shoes and clothing soon were undertaken.

Some members, who did not agree with any policy that looked ahead, grumbled, particularly because the dividend then being paid was not as high as they wished [the chronicle reads]. Members who thought the enterprise was heading for the rocks left the society. One of the anxious ones withdrew about £40 of his capital from the society and invested it in a colliery company which collapsed in a few months. Learning a lesson from his loss, he soon became a more staunch co-operator.

With 29,000 members, this society now does an annual business of $6,670,000, paying a dividend of 1 shilling 3 pence for each £1 of trade. It owns a 686-acre dairy farm and supplies 90 per cent of the town's milk. This people's big business that once was transported in a handcart now has 115 selling points, including chemists shops and traveling grocery vans.

There are larger groups, and there are smaller, but it is fairly representative of what a well-managed co-operative can accomplish. As in most other instances the commercial service is paralleled by cultural and educational activities ranging from lecture courses to choirs and dramatic groups.

Constant pressure is exerted by members here and there for more rapid expansion of services. Price restrictions by the British oil interests which do not permit co-op refunds have discouraged development of co-op services to automobile owners such as in the United States. Newcastle and a few other co-ops provide gasoline for a membership in which car ownership is not general. Several of the larger societies service their fleets of trucks with co-op oil from the United States.

In one city a co-op member who rides a motorcycle to his work as a school gardener heads a movement for a repair and equipment service which may eventually develop. His vocation leads him also to advocate the buying out of a local nursery to supply at less cost the shrubs and plants so characteristic of the English scene.

Meanwhile each Tuesday throngs of co-op retail managers and

buyers mill around CWS salesrooms in Manchester, London and other centers. Lining the curb outside these showrooms are salesmen representing private traders seeking the crumbs of co-op business orders. These hangers-on seek to buttonhole representatives of the consumer interest as they leave headquarters. There have been, of course, instances of commercial bribery. No effort is spared to induce local co-op purchasing agents to give more trade to outside interests in preference to their own plants.

One Scottish board of directors, informed by its manager of the offer of a watch and a rug by a factory agent seeking preferential treatment, advised him to accept the gifts and put them in the co-op stock for sale.

### 4. VOLUNTARY OR COMPULSORY PROGRESS?

The human element is uppermost in co-operation; consequently it reflects no single viewpoint but the varied views of the men and women it serves. Most co-operators seem still to want an alternative method to the capitalist system. They believe that co-operative services provide the best alternative. As consumers they realize that in the fight against monopolies the co-ops and the government must work together.

They believe also that many common needs can be better served by state or municipal action than under the profit system. Nevertheless, they are unwilling to see their own co-operative systems supplanted by bureaucratic public controls in which the human element is missing.

A statement issued by the Co-operative Union expresses the belief that "a democratic society will not apply the principle of compulsion to any part of the economic field where the voluntary principle already succeeds."

A later pamphlet, *Social Ownership and Consumer Problems*, stakes out the claim that the co-ops themselves constitute a form of social ownership. "Democracy will prosper only if it learns to use every agency created by the people to advance the cause of social justice and equality," the statement goes. "These agencies, created by its own efforts, must be fully utilized as part of the process by which the social ideals of democracy are realized." I put this issue to Viscount Alexander of Hillsborough, long a prominent figure in the co-operative movement. As A. V. Alexander he came to public service through the co-ops, having been parliamentary secretary of the Co-operative Union. He became First Lord of the Admiralty in Winston Churchill's wartime cabinet and was Minister of Defense in the postwar Labour government.

"Co-operation is 100 per cent social ownership," he told me as we came out of the Manchester headquarters of the Co-operative Wholesale Society. Having retired to his farm in Essex, he returns now and then to renew his contacts with the social force that started him on a notable career. We paused near Balloon Street, the nerve center of the British movement. It was in the late afternoon, and the first wave of the 3,000 men and women employees was rolling out of its various office buildings and warehouses. Here are the executive quarters of CWS, and across a narrow way is the CWS bank, sixth largest financial institution in the country. A handsome building with a curved front at the head of the street is the seat of the Co-operative Insurance Society, second in volume of industrial policies. Up nearby Hanover street is Holyoake House, the central office of the Co-operative Union.

"There is no finer training for the responsibilities of citizenship than service in a democratic, voluntary organization like the co-operative movement," Viscount Alexander remarked. "One valuable thing it does is stressing the responsibilities of freedom as well as its privileges. Look at these great buildings around us —who owns them? Not any group of stockholders, but the British people, with new owners joining constantly of their own accord. I say this is an outstanding form of the freest of free enterprise, in which the social interest is uppermost."

Still the co-operative idea has yet to receive the attention politically, and even as a social and economic factor, that the number and the massed power of its supporters would seem to warrant.

A plea for wider recognition and application of the principles involved was conveyed to the 1953 Trade Union Congress by C. E. Wolf, representing the Co-operative Union. "You have on your doorsteps co-operatives which are capable of all the advantages of public ownership without the troublesome business of legislation," he declared.

In the debate that followed the trade union delegates recommended that the Labour party go slow in planning further nationalization, pending study of results with the mines and railways. The resolution to this effect was introduced by Patrick Geddes, general secretary of the Union of Post Office Workers, who cited his experience in forty years with the public postal and communication service. Acknowledging that a substantial majority opinion may still hold that the mere act of nationalization would bring every benefit to the people and remove existing evils, he warned that no one is quite so autocratic as a "well-instructed civil servant."

The Labour party conference opening later at Margate reflected a similar spirit of wait-and-see. Final resolutions were confined to a demand merely for the nationalization of the water supply, plus a recommendation for the study of the industrial insurance business with an eye to more economical mutual or public operation.

This fell short of unifying the elements making up Labour party strength. Particularly it was a setback for Aneurin Bevan's left-wing proposal to absorb the chemical industry and also to nationalize the land. Impatient supporters of Bevan quote him as saying: "Are you prepared to encourage the growth of the economic jungle until such time as the co-operatives are ready to cut it down?"

One of the outstanding directors of the CWS, J. W. Peddie, had delivered unusually pointed fraternal greetings to the Labour party conference. The tenor of his address, though conciliatory, was obviously influenced by the omission of any reference to the place of consumer co-operation in future society in the party's campaign document, *Challenge to Britain.* "We have no intention of allowing ourselves to be the central figure of our own funeral, no matter how friendly the undertaker may be," he warned the convention.

Seated at a long table extending across the stage were former Prime Minister Attlee, Bevan and other figures of the late Labour government. Seizing this opportunity Mr. Peddie spoke of co-operation as an important and promising form of social ownership, and not to be overlooked. He went on to say that some might believe that co-operative enterprises were simply a useful prelude to the development of some system of state control that was destined to take them over. Wrong and dangerous, he called that idea.

Later Mr. Peddie told me that he did not believe that British working men and women would have found courage to run a government if they had not first learned how to conduct a business of their own. Success in co-operative shopkeeping, manufacture, insurance and banking has engendered confidence and self-reliance. Democratic processes thus have been made real through experience and personal service. Particularly in a welfare state any stimulant of individual spirit has high social value. Freedom itself may depend on the next step, collective working in voluntary association.

To Mr. Peddie the mere ability to cast a ballot does not assure democracy. Apart from election day, citizens have daily responsibilities also in economic areas involving such matters as conditions of employment and the standard of living. The pressure of the example set by the co-operative movement has brought about numerous reforms. The eight-hour day was pioneered in the co-op biscuit factory, half-day closing in the co-op shops, which also led in applying the principle of collective bargaining with organized labor, a field in which the rest of the distributive business houses still lag.

No matter for surprise, then, that the Co-operative party program has dovetailed with that of the Labour party, their candidates never opposing each other. The new estrangement between the advocates of swift compulsion and slower voluntary progress is not at all to the distress of the Conservative party.

A Co-operative parliamentary candidate with the joint sponsorship of the Labour party brought back from a political briefing at the Margate conference the impression that many Labour party leaders are almost completely ignorant of the co-operative world. The intellectuals, including most of the Fabian Society, have had practically no experience with the stores and services. On the other hand, the skilled artisans and the thrifty section of the working class that built the co-ops are outnumbered by newer unions of the unskilled. The latter are less familiar with the theory and practice of consumer action, and instead place their entire hope in the predominance of the producer interest.

"People who think as producers rather than as consumers are bound to develop fragmentary interests," Secretary Jacques told me at Portsmouth. "Work must be viewed as means to an end—and that end is consumption. What we can buy with our wages after we get them is an important question. As consumers we can be as one, but as producers we are divided. Indeed, there are trade unions that spend a good deal of time just scrapping with each other in jurisdictional disputes. How much better as a basis of democracy is a common purpose of plenty for all."

Mr. Jacques confirmed the impression of rising doubts over Labour party policy, which seemed to be leaning backward to avoid any appearance of favoring the co-ops, even in the assignment of local facilities for shops in new housing developments. At the same time Co-operative parliamentarians are left with only a hazy idea of any definite political line since most co-operative thinking concentrates on problems of trade.

A courageous and clear-cut position is that of Jack Bailey, secretary of the Co-operative party, who seeks to bring about a better political understanding. Socialists, he says, must learn to think more of the people and less of the state as an instrument of social change. The consumer view is thus outlined in his pamphlet contribution to a Labour party educational series:

Co-operators in the country have built up for themselves, and for all who wish to join them, an integrated economy from baker's shop to flour mill, from tea table to tea plantation. Each activity of the co-operative movement—milk, transport, insurance, selling preserves over the counter and making them in a co-operative factory—is linked up with all the other trading activities. To break the chain is to disturb the co-operative economy and to destroy the co-operative system.

A somewhat different approach is that of Prof. G. D. H. Cole, the noted economist who is president of the Fabian Society. Almost alone among British social scientists, he has written a great deal on the various aspects of co-operative theory and practice. In the *Review of International Co-operation* he writes as follows:

As I have followed the course of discussions in this country between the Labour party and the Co-operative Movement concerning the extent and character of plans for nationalization of industry, my thoughts have turned again and again to the future of producers' co-operation. Not so the thoughts of most of the British co-operative leaders, any more than those who think out ahead the policies of the Labour party and of the Trade Unions.

More recently Prof. Cole has seen fit to issue a warning that co-operatives must not become a buffer for capitalism. In his book *The British Co-operative Movement in a Socialist Society*, he says that unless the movement matches up to its opportunities the state will be driven to take over enterprises otherwise better suited to co-operative development.

I gathered in conversation with him that this threat had been designed to spur co-operative expansion, which under wartime controls had been reined in. His low regard for co-operative leadership, except in certain local areas, was undisguised. The way should be opened, he said, for college graduates to find the same opportunity for employment in the co-ops that is given them in profit industry.

The question why there had not been more research into the connotations of the consumer movement as a social and eco-

nomic force brought the offhand response that it was because the
subject was so dull. Occasionally Dr. Cole collaborates with his
wife, who is a prolific author of mystery novels, which have a
much different standard from that of the once dismal science of
economics. But in a detective story there is doubt until the last
moment over who-dun-it. Whereas in a co-op—well, no mystery
about that; we-all-dun-it.

Later, addressing a Fabian meeting at the time of the Labour
party conference, Dr. Cole began by saying that what his country most needed was leaders who were not afraid to voice un-
popular ideas. In his criticism of Labour party tactics he did not
mention any aspect of co-operation. He expressed the belief that
Great Britain under Labour government had made a mistake in
soliciting American financial aid; he expressed misgivings over
British entry into Korean fighting; and as the next step for
nationalization he suggested the building industry, basic to meeting the need for housing, hospitals and schools.

It has remained for a Durham University economist, P. R.
Kaim-Caudle, to suggest a system of national shops to compete
with co-ops and private traders. This proposal evoked considerable questioning when he addressed a co-op educational conference at Newcastle. The national shops, he explained, would
not have to do much trade; the knowledge that one could be
opened anywhere might keep prices down. As experiments in
municipal business he recommended coal and milk distribution,
in which local authorities would have a monopoly.

The *Co-operative News* commented that there is nothing new
in these ideas. Its reply for the co-op movement is unchanged:
that competition of any kind is welcomed provided it is fair. But
if state shops are to be subsidized out of taxes the movement
would oppose them.

What is most feared is business control of government, and not
government control of a largely monopolized economic system.
Some opportunity is seen for the co-ops and the government to
work together in behalf of a mixed economy making available
the abundance of goods and service which modern technology
stands ready to provide.

# [ III ]

# STRAIGHT LINE DISTRIBUTION

## 1. For All the World to See

THE magnetic pull of the idea of production for use instead of profit draws pilgrims from all quarters of the world. Particularly those peoples only now emerging toward industrialism are sending delegations to explore British co-operative success.

Certain advantages from the integration of production and distribution are apparent. For one, the speculative element is held at a minimum as co-operative factories are producing for a known demand. Some of the waste of making goods before finding buyers for them has been eliminated.

The existence of a loyal body of patron-members simplifies the problem of mass distribution. Not only are consumers spared high pressure sales methods which force on them unwanted goods or things they cannot afford, but they are not exposed to other unhealthy trade practices.

Consumer control of retail stores has made possible a smooth flow of distribution all the way from the original sources. Thus, back of the retail co-ops are eleven CWS shoe factories which in turn draw leather from co-op tanneries which treat the hides from co-op slaughterhouses. Six CWS plants make men's and boys' outerwear, including "be-spoke" or made-to-measure garments. The society's own mills supply a large proportion of the 2,000,000 yards of wool cloth, the 1,500,000 yards of cotton goods and the 250,000 yards of rayon. These textile works draw their yarn from CWS spinning plants, completing an unbroken chain.

In a year more than 55,000 visitors, mainly from local retail societies, make co-op factory tours. One such party was made up of members of the Young Farmers of Cheshire and their wives, brought to Manchester in two motor coaches belonging to the Chester co-op. A day of sightseeing opened in the great flour mill strategically located on the ship canal by which grain cargoes from overseas are delivered directly to its bins. Here the Young Farmers saw their own wheat mixed with that from Canada, the United States and Australia. As members of Chester co-op, they buy back the by-product for dairy feed.

The process of vertical integration includes many bakeries making bread from co-op flour. Some of these are operated by single co-operatives, as in Chester, Derby and London, and others by regional federations. The simple logic by which an enterprise owns the plants which produce the raw materials it uses is readily recognized. The many advantages, including the reduction of cost, are particularly appealing to overseas deputations seeking a pattern for lands as yet undeveloped.

Here was a party from Pakistan—each man with a compass to orient his prayers in the direction of Mecca. They found on arrival in Manchester that quite differently all roads lead to the economic shrines of the people in business. On a conducted tour to the soap works at nearby Irlam we drove past five other factories of the Co-operative Wholesale Society and dozens of retail outlets. Down one street in Manchester the guide pointed out the CWS tobacco works. Across the bridge at Salford a glass factory was turning out milk bottles and medicine vials by the millions. In a back street along the way we paused at a newly acquired plant making women's rayon vests. A twine and rope mill and the huge margarine factory at High Irlam completed the day's list.

Another party visiting the soap works included a Sudanese student completing a year at the Co-operative College, a Nigerian fresh from study of municipal government at Cambridge University, a young Swedish co-operative employee and another from the Netherlands.

The first impression of the soap plant is of a modern glass-sided building set back in a green lawn and a flowering garden. An assistant manager comes out to meet the tourists and introduces the guide, a young woman in a white smock. The young Sudanese jots down copious notes of the soap-making process, whether for a college examination or for use on his return home to Africa is not clear. I find myself noting down such facts as . . . 850 employees . . . seventy-ton mixture in two-story vat . . . packaging Christmas boxes of pink, blue and white toilet soaps . . . Australian tallow . . . African palm oil.

The development of synthetic detergents as a supplement for soap has opened a new trade war. Not to be behind, the co-ops are producing an excellent product called "Spel" in a three-cornered merchandising free-for-all with a British combine and an American corporation seeking a new market. In a flanking movement the chief chemist at Irlam is even experimenting with sound waves as a method of removing dirt from clothing. Meanwhile the free offers, the gift coupons, the repeated claims and ballyhoo of the private concerns have confused many consumers. Some societies, as in London, have refused to stock any other than co-op brands.

Even some of the co-op counterhands appear bewildered over the relative merits of what actually is a standardized chemical formula. The CWS market research department has acquired a wire recording of one shopping experience.

"Have you a detergent powder?" a patron asks.

"We have only Spel," the young woman clerk replies. "But I think Tide is the best. You can buy that in the store across the street."

Regionally federated co-operative laundries are financed by groups of retail societies. This typically co-operative method of pooling capital and sharing risks for wider consumer services extends also in large-scale dairies and bakeries as well as in the field of newspaper and magazine publication.

On a national scale the retail groups join to maintain the Co-operative Wholesale Society. Created more than ninety years ago as a buying agency for the local co-ops, it has expanded into production. CWS factories now produce one-third of the goods sold by retail co-ops. Investment funds find opportunity in banking, insurance and home loans. A subsidiary, Travco, operates twelve hotels, chiefly in holiday areas, and a travel agency.

Paralleling CWS is the Scottish Co-operative Wholesale Society, also owned and controlled by member co-ops, some of them agricultural rather than industrial. There also are some individual Scottish shareholders, among them employees. Wholesale directors are elected by the societies holding shares, voting in proportion to their purchases rather than to their financial holdings.

Top management of CWS consists of a board of twenty-eight. These directors are elected on a regional basis by postal votes from the management committees of affiliated societies. After four years' service they come up for re-election, and having gained in experience usually are kept in office. Quarterly meetings of CWS correspond to the membership meetings of retail co-ops, with cross-questioning of the executive staff, largely on matters of efficiency and supply. Regional offices, each with extensive salesrooms, are at Newcastle, Cardiff and Bristol in addition to London and Manchester.

CWS sales have doubled in six years, at last reports running at the rate of $1,178,000,000 a year. The newest of its seven flour mills, at London's Royal Victoria dock, is one of the most modern in Europe, and Sun mills at Manchester are the largest. About 15 per cent of all flour ground in Britain comes from CWS.

A documentary film frequently shown for propaganda purposes links the local co-op with this massive productive development. It is one of a series designed for showing in halls above stores and even in daylight open-air locations.

Seen first is a shopping crowd entering a co-op, the narrator explaining: "The co-operative way of trading differs from other ways by being undertaken for the benefit of the customer. . . . Anyone can join and become a member, customer, owner and controller all in one.

"The co-op exists to buy everything—from tea to a flatiron; from mangles to margarine—and to sell them to its own members. Businesses of the other sort exist to pay profits to their owners. The customers own the co-op, therefore it is the customer who gets the benefit of co-operative trading."

The scene shifts to a membership meeting and then to an overall view of a furniture factory which spreads over several acres. The voice speaks of the connection of the retail co-ops with manufacture:

"They have baked biscuits and made shoes ever since 1873.

"They have been milling flour ever since 1891.

"And weaving cloth ever since 1876."

The enumeration goes on from bedding to cigarettes, nail brushes and pins. In the Yorkshire town where the mobile cinema is playing is a CWS ironworks. Originally designed to make clothes wringers, it now has progressed to washing machines, spring mattresses, metal chairs and stepladders. There also the Keighley Industrial Co-operative Society, more than ninety years old, has 14,000 members in a population of 56,000, with sales for the half year exceeding $1,500,000.

The advantages of the co-operative setup were not overlooked by the commission which President Franklin D. Roosevelt sent to Europe in 1937. In its report of the inquiry into co-operative enterprise is an appendix dealing with the uninterrupted flow of goods to the consumer. The statement is made: "Each point at which this distributive process is interrupted by speculative bargaining represents economic waste." The finding is demonstrated by a chart presented by Hugo Vasarla, managing director of the Finnish co-operative SOK. It was he who made plain to the American inquiry that sound economies are achieved, not by paying lower wages in the distributive trades, but by effecting a continuous and orderly movement of goods from producer to consumer. Where distribution goes largely unorganized the line is first broken by private jobbers, then by private wholesale organizations. Then come unorganized retailers, selling to unorganized consumers. Slightly more rationalization appears among retailers organized to operate their own wholesale establishment, sometimes as a dealer co-operative. But when the consumers own the retail shops, Vasarla said, there is uninterrupted control and consequent economy. In England CWS has pioneered in rationalizing all these functions from the raw material to the finished garment.

The co-operative movement for all its success has not lost any of the pace-setting functions that gave it its original impetus. What may seem to the casual observer to have become only another huge trading machine sparked by some non-existent special advantage in the way of taxation or political favoritism will be seen on closer examination as a stabilizing influence.

Existing side by side with other forms of trading it continues to act as a deterrent to exorbitant prices. Bakeries operated by the co-ops, and using CWS flour were able to break a bread ring, as reported by the Royal Food Commission in 1925. An investigating committee found that local associations of master bakers had attempted to fix prices through "coercive and dictatorial methods which are not only reprehensible in themselves, but clearly detrimental to the public interest."

Here was a case in which addition of a penny on the loaf would have raised the people's bread bill by $28,000,000. But, in the words of the Royal Commission: "The loss to the public from price-fixing arrangements in the baking trade is not likely to be serious in those districts where the co-operative societies pursue an independent policy directed toward keeping bread prices as low as possible."

The British Ministry of Food in 1951 authorized a charge of threepence a week for home delivery of bread. When the great London Co-operative Society refused to tax consumers thus, its competitors did not even attempt to impose the charge on their customers.

The Labour government in an effort to halt inflation appealed to merchants to reduce prices in 1948. The co-operative movement responded by cuts on all rationed goods. In the London Society alone margins were narrowed by $185,000. In spite of this considerable aggregate, the saving to patrons per unit of purchase was trifling. Furthermore, under the rationing regulations it was impossible for consumers to shift their buying from whatever shop in which they had originally registered. While the co-ops were supplying one out of each four families with rationed foods, the rest were tied to private dealers, and the price cut was abandoned.

The war with its shortages brought in many substitutes and improvisations for such scarce items as lemons, onions and eggs. In an order designed to check fraud, the Minister of Food in 1941 prohibited manufacture of food substitutes except under license. Corn flour and oatmeal had been sold as egg powder; wheat flour, gelatin and common salt as milk powder substitute and plain flour as Yorkshire pudding mixture. One "egg powder" that sold at shilling twopence a packet was said to be "as much like egg substitute as the office gum pot."

A rush of prosecutions deflated this ersatz boom. Although a number of prepared mixtures have been made by the co-operative wholesales, hardly any changes had to be made to conform to the newly imposed standards. From the beginning a basic Rochdale principle was selling pure food and giving honest measure at fair prices. One of the first ventures of CWS was grinding pepper, this at the insistence of the retail societies troubled over adulteration.

Here is a conscientious force standing for the homely virtues by which men grow in moral stature and understanding. Outside all the dodges of sharp dealing and the makeshifts of political legerdemain, the co-operatives give precedence to human welfare, overcoming the limitations of the individual without submerging any of the rights of man—costing only the renunciation of the privilege of exploiting one another.

## 2. Londoners Get Together

In all the world there is no duplicate of the London Co-operative Society, the largest of five enterprises by which consumers serve themselves in the complex composing the British capital. Its membership in round numbers is 1,150,000, and as many as 1,000 new shareholders sign up in a week. Housewives compose half of the management committee. Annual trade exceeds $135,000,000, and each year at least $5,000,000 is refunded on members' purchases. There are 19,000 employees and 1,200 trading points including 365 grocery shops and 99 dry goods stores.

The repetition of statistics can become meaningless except as they are interpreted. Reassuring from the American standpoint is the evidence that large city populations have proved themselves capable of working together toward a common end. Service and convenience, low competitive prices and the refund on purchases have built LCS. With a well-established demand as a backlog it is able to do considerable processing and manufacturing on its own. Its workshops make furniture, upholstery and bedding. It operates laundries, bakes bread and has a dairy supplying a weekly total of 5,500,000 pints of milk.

"We don't know all the answers even yet," said E. W. Shopland, the president. He indicated his observations on a visit of inspection to the United States with other board members. "Unlike America, co-ops here got their start before the days of what you call chain stores, and of the supermarkets. The small shop is done, even as a beginning, and you must start large enough to develop mass buying power. One thing well to be considered is the one-stop shopping center such as I have seen in the United States. A fundamental consideration must be the buyers' needs and convenience, not the seller's interest. Let's face the facts, dividends do play an important part, though there are other values. It would be a rather sad thing if there was nothing else."

Most small co-ops do not offer such low prices as LCS, although many exceed its dividend rate of tenpence on the pound, less than the national average. Variations in margins, turnover, pensions, taxes, reserves, educational, political and charitable grants, bonuses to employees and collective life insurance policies all affect the net surplus which is refunded. In the older co-ops of Northern England and of Scotland, housewives traditionally have looked upon the dividend as a means of accumulating savings, and therefore have not expected competitive prices, let alone price cutting. There has been a downward trend in these refunds reflecting price controls, heavy taxes and in some cases a more active pricing policy.

It seems that dividends are not so important as they used to be, for even as they tend down, membership continues to go up. Before the war the annual dividend might be £10 per member, about two weeks' wages in those days. Today the refund is nearer £8, at current wage scales closer to four days' wages.

LCS savings of a penny a glass on the price of table jellies, twopence on cake flour, a halfpenny on sandwich spread and a farthing on coffee essence may seem inconsequential to all except thrifty or necessitous housewives. Larger advantages appear in proprietary drugs, where price maintenance is practiced in private trade. CWS aspirin is only a shilling, or 14 cents, for one hundred tablets, as against two shillings sevenpence (36 cents) for the main advertised brand. One hundred halibut oil capsules at four shillings twopence represent a saving of more than half. Co-operators buy four ounces of hand cream for two shillings; elsewhere the same coins buy only a two-and-a-half-ounce bottle.

A research and testing laboratory is maintained by LCS. Its chemists have found that a bottle of liquid laundry blue that competitors were selling at eleven pence halfpenny contained only 0.5 per cent of bluing, the contents being worth less than one-twelfth of a penny.

Alone among all commercial enterprises co-operation has everything to gain and nothing to fear from an informed buying public. On the positive side the co-ops stand for sanitary handling and adequate labeling of goods. Their dairies meet the highest standards under a system of ownership that diminishes the necessity for official controls and inspection. People in the business of supplying their own needs are under no temptation to profit by dubious methods. In addition to a higher standard of living, Rochdale co-operation has always aimed at a rising level of understanding.

In London a multitude of opportunities is offered members to study the history and economics of the movement and otherwise to fit themselves for civic leadership or promotion on the job if they are employees. Out of this process of further education have risen not only business executives but statesmen as well.

The seventh child of a docker in the East End was the first president of LCS. When eight years old he lost his left leg in a fairgrounds accident. At fourteen he entered evening classes in metal design and in five years was doing delicate gold and silver work. Upon reaching voting age he joined the Independent Labour party, his trade union and Stratford co-op, where eighteen months later he was president. Upon amalgamation of his own and other small societies into LCS he continued as president. In time of depression he protected the staff from dismissal and persuaded members to forgo dividends in order to keep jobs open.

Such were the beginnings of the Right Hon. Alfred Barnes, successively a Member of Parliament, Junior Lord of the Treasury and national chairman of the Co-operative party. And in 1945, when the Labour government took over the British railways, it was he who piloted the Transport Nationalization bill through Parliament.

The consumer movement in London has been in close alliance with the Labour party. A Baptist minister, the Rev. W. Thomas Williams, elected on the Labour and Co-operative party ticket, represents South Hammersmith in Parliament. A university teacher, educated at Oxford, he was a wartime chaplain and welfare officer in the Royal Air Force.

Two other clergymen are among the lecturers for the Women's Co-operative Guilds of LCS. The Rev. W. Long speaks on the career of Robert Owen, one of those who sowed the first seeds of co-operation. The Rev. Stanley Evans of the Church of England has as his topic the influence of William Morris.

"The British co-operative movement grew out of desperately poor working people learning to help each other for their common good, and to protect themselves from perpetual efforts to capitalize on their misery," the Rev. Mr. Evans said. "It hardly need be stressed that these objectives are utterly Christian, and that Christian support of the co-operatives is an elementary exercise in the basic Biblical principle that we are our brother's keepers."

He cited an archbishops' report indorsing co-operation for public service and not competition for private gain as the true principle of industry, and finds it no accident that Christians played a significant part in the beginning. He continued: "The Christian Socialist movement, as it was called, associated with the name of Frederick Denison Maurice, Charles Kingsley and others, was interested in co-operation from the start. When the first Co-operative Congress was called in 1869, the provisional summons included three of the great names of Christian Socialism, J. N. Ludlow, E. Vansittart Neale and Thomas Hughes. They had supported the movement throughout, as their successors do to this day."

A memorial tablet in the crypt of St. Paul's cathedral pays this tribute to Mr. Neale, the first secretary of the Co-operative Union, who died in 1892:

> HE NEITHER POWER NOR RICHES SOUGHT,
> FOR OTHERS, NOT HIMSELF, HE FOUGHT.

Above his bearded image is the co-operative imperative, "Labour and Wait," and below the simple statement, "Unity Is Strength." In the dedicatory exercises the dean of St. Paul's took the text, "Bear ye one another's burdens, and so fulfill the law of Christ."

Neale, the son of a clergyman, and himself a wealthy member of the bar, laid the legal foundation for co-operation and expended a considerable share of his own means in support of producer co-operation. He visited America in 1875 with a delegation seeking direct trade between Western farmers and the English co-operatives.

His successor in the Co-operative Union was his friend, Judge Thomas Hughes, author of *Tom Brown's School Days*. An unsuccessful attempt by Hughes to establish a co-operative community of impoverished English younger sons at Rugby, Tennessee, matched in some respects Owen's settlement at New Harmony, Indiana.

Prominent also among the Christian Socialists was the Rev. Charles Kingsley, best known for his novel, *Westward Ho!* rather than for his association with the brilliant group who found an answer for the social problem in the teachings of Christ.

The emphasis that this philanthropic movement had given to co-operative production and to profit sharing in industry gradually was shifted under the pressures of financial losses from self-governing workshops. By the nineties of the last century J. W. T. Mitchell, a Rochdaler who had become chairman of CWS, had discovered the pre-eminence of the consumer.

"I want no laws to be passed to divide anybody's property," he told the Co-operative Congress. "What I want is for co-operators, trades unionists and all the industrious classes of this and every other country, to combine in keeping their own shop, making a good dividend, producing, distributing and financing, and let all the profits come to those who consume the goods, because they have made them."

The change of direction, which was not without considerable heartbreak, is told with all sympathy by Horace M. Kallen in his book *The Decline and Rise of the Consumer*. Sorting out means from ends, co-operators have learned that production is for man, not man for production. A statement such as this needs telling until it becomes a part of Western culture.

Out of their trading surplus co-ops finance classes and study groups of many kinds. Each month LCS invests $10,000 in educational, cultural and social activities. Young people are organized to play together, choral groups are trained to sing together, and lectures, film forums and discussions help members to think together. The final achievement, acting together, is realized in the guilds and on the various committees.

The marvel is that an institution as huge as LCS is able to foster the spirit of neighborliness, this in the world's largest city. Local committees watch over assigned areas, receive complaints and make recommendations to the management.

Another example of neighborliness is the arrangement making sickroom appliances available on loan to members. Each district committee appoints a custodian from among its group of six men and women, to serve without fee. Thus are supplied invalid chairs, backrests, hot water bottles, bedpans, rubber sheets and air cushions, at a nominal charge covering costs of delivery and cleaning.

A convalescent fund also is maintained by a deduction of one-pence per member per year. Beneficiaries are asked to pay their own fare to one of nineteen available rest homes if possible, in addition to $1.40 per week. In case of dire need, these benefits are free. The usual length of stay is two weeks, with the possibility of a longer period when found advisable.

When families are bereaved, LCS like many smaller societies promptly makes a cash payment based on average purchases, this through arrangement with the Co-operative Insurance Society. "That £18 funeral bonus was a Godsend when money was most needed," a widow interviewed among other shoppers in the outlying village of Onger said. No premium collection, age limit or medical examination is involved.

Survivors are not likely to bargain over the cost of a proper funeral, and here, too, the co-op protects its members. It was in 1944 that a Conservative reform committee reported "that often the first inquiry is liable to be 'How much have you to spend?' and the funeral is liable to be fixed at that figure." On the other hand, even before the war the Scottish Co-operative Wholesale Society had reduced funeral prices by one-third. With this as a gauge of costs, government intervention in 1949 reached an agreement with the funeral furnishing business for a maximum charge of about $60 for a simple funeral with coffin, hearse and one following car, with four bearers. Now one-fourth of all funerals is under co-operative auspices, and at Rugby the co-op conducts 71 per cent of burials. Approximately 7,000 funerals are managed by LCS in a year. In the same period it paid approximately $300,000 in 12,000 death claims. At its Manor Park industrial site there is not only a coffin-making works and a funeral chapel but also a monumental masonry department, as it is called. Everything from gravestones to flowers and a funeral fleet of Daimler automobiles is available through twenty-four undertaking branches.

But it is for the living that London Co-operative functions, with such developments as a new housing development with 5,000 homes, its summer camps for children, the residential weekend schools at Hollybank, its choirs, orchestras and drama groups. In saying that its primary purpose is consumer welfare, the values are moral and ethical as well as economic.

### 3. FARM TO TABLE

Agricultural co-operation has been much slower to take root in Great Britain than in the United States, where it is a major force. However, when English farm organizations have needed help they have been able to rely on the consumer movement for aid not forthcoming through commercial channels.

Although some leaders of American farm co-ops incline to the feeling that consumer groups have no other purpose than to buy cheaply, actual practice shows that both can benefit by close relations. Certainly it is to the advantage of rural and urban interests alike to reduce costs of production and distribution. Joint services and trading involving the agricultural co-operatives and the Co-operative Wholesale Society have a record of success.

The assets of many rural groups were swamped in 1924 by the failure of an Agricultural Wholesale Society set up five years before as a farm supply co-operative. In this emergency CWS salvaged the wreckage and bailed out several local farmer ventures. This friendly attitude was in contrast to the hostility and even boycott experienced at the hands of established profit enterprise.

Out of 300 farm co-ops in England and Wales, 104 are members of CWS, participating in its meetings and sharing in patronage refunds. A further 31, though not members, make purchases through the Wholesale Society. Only 5, however, have affiliated with the Co-operative Union.

It appears that British farmers prefer to tie themselves to state action through marketing boards which control distribution and guarantee prices. The National Farmers' Union has developed into a political pressure group entirely out of sympathy with the political alliance of the consumers in the Co-operative party.

Looking to the complete decontrol of foodstuffs, CWS has maintained its buying depots in the United States, Canada, Argentine, Australia, New Zealand and Denmark. In addition the society owns a large freezing works in New Zealand and is joint owner of another with a dairy co-op there. Two bacon factories in Denmark also are held by CWS. In West Australia hard-pressed farm organizations have CWS to thank for support against unfriendly financial and market interests. When wheat growers there were unable to get proper terms from the banks for co-operative marketing, CWS advanced a total of £18,-000,000 through nine harvests.

It required two wars and the German submarines to register the importance of a home-grown food supply. With an area only equivalent to that of the state of Idaho and a population eighty-five times as large, Britain now produces 40 per cent of its own food. Until recently food subsidies have really been subsidies to the consumer, since during the period of war, blockade and dollar shortage the limited home supplies would have brought nearly famine prices if some of the costs had not been borne through taxes. Now that food once more is available on the world market at lower prices than those promised to the home farmer, the subsidy obviously is going to the farmer, not the consumer. More than ever is the need for common understanding that artificially maintained high prices tend to decrease consumption to an extent ultimately menacing farm income.

Recognition of the benefits of two-way trade is represented by a joint committee on agricultural and consumer co-operation. Since 1924 CWS has been the only important co-operative source of farm machinery, feed, seed, fertilizer, rope, twine and paint. Its horticultural department at Derby tests, develops and imports farm seeds. These are cleaned and examined for germination qualities in the consumer-owned laboratory. A more recent development is a large fertilizer works jointly owned with farm co-operatives.

Outstanding as an example of mutual association is the Derby retail co-op's relation with some 300 market gardeners in the Vale of Evesham. They are organized in their own co-operative, the Littleton and Badsey Growers Ltd., in which the Derby consumer co-op has an investment of $1,500. Before the day of wartime price fixing the retail society handled these small growers' fruit and market produce on open invoice, prices being adjusted later. Now prices are arranged by telephone. The seed potatoes bought from the retail co-op come back as food to the same society, of which the farmers also are members. The farm co-op in turn holds membership in CWS and the Co-operative Union.

The most striking aspect of this arrangement is that the Derby consumers, 100,000 strong, own two farms and operate a huge dairy business as well as their own egg-grading station.

Consumer co-operatives farm more than 62,000 acres in Britain. From these come considerable amounts of milk, bacon and other meat, vegetables, fruit, poultry and eggs. One orchard acquired by CWS from a bankrupt promotion contains 1,600,000 apple trees, requiring spraying by helicopter. Another CWS tract supplies fruit for its jam factories.

Some of these consumer-owned farms are show places, better equipped than most individual operations. This ownership of crop land, which until recent years was far from profitable, has served to acquaint city-bred management committees with agricultural problems. Even now there is a tendency to dispose of what is regarded as an uncertain asset. One society after thirty-eight years has sold its livestock and leased its acreage. Another sale of a dairy farm acquired years ago resulted from growth of the milk business to five times its output.

Some American farm co-operators look askance at the British consumer establishment because of an uneasy feeling over these experiments in food production. But consumer holdings constitute a small proportion of the United Kingdom's 530,000 farms and 31,000,000 acres of cultivated land. Their annual production, less interest and depreciation, is estimated at $10,000,000 including 29,000 acres reported by CWS.

It is not easy to distinguish a farm owned by a consumer co-op from one of the corporation farms that are multiplying in the United States. Operations may be as efficient as in a factory, but even well-paid labor does not feel the incentive that springs naturally from the soil of family-type farms.

One able manager who was leaving a large co-op holding to run an individually owned hop farm commented on this handicap as we drove by the trim cottages occupied by families of farm laborers. There are more than fifty persons on this farm staff, including seven wives or daughters useful with the milking machines or in the pasteurization process. Their general well-being was indicated by small automobiles in three of the cottage yards. But to the manager these spoke also of a desire to get away from rural life and hunt pleasure in town.

"These people would take much more interest in their work if they could have some share in the ownership of the land," the manager confessed.

A report to the 1953 Co-operative Congress by the Central Executive notes that some societies have recently disposed of farms, usually at an attractive figure. It adds this conclusion: "In the light of returns from distributive activities the societies concerned could fully justify withdrawing from possible liabilities of the future maintenance of their farms and utilizing the capital arising for other purposes more in line with the general business of the societies."

With a view to bridging over this economic divide, the International Co-operative Alliance has recommended linking the two forms of co-operation by joint enterprises, particularly in the field of processing and marketing agricultural produce. An example often cited as reconciling the interests of buyers and sellers is that at Geneva, Switzerland. There the milk-collecting points are owned by farmers' co-operatives, the distributive rounds by consumers' co-operatives and the central pasteurizing and bottling plant by a joint organization of the two.

In the ICA discussion Norman Wood of CWS referred to the social as well as commercial values in an organized approach to the problem of a just price. A delegate of the French National Federation of Agricultural Co-operation, J. Fauchon, spoke of the possibility of stabilizing prices and curbing speculation by long-term consumer-producer agreements. In his opinion it could be less important for agricultural producers to have high prices at certain times and low prices at others than to produce a steady supply at a stable price.

While the consumer movement is not tending toward wider agricultural fields, organized farmers are moving into processing their own crops and manufacturing for their own requirements. Producers are discussing cold storage to avoid gluts, quick freezing to ensure continuity of supply. A Scottish fruit-marketing co-op now operates a sweet and jam factory in the Moray Firth region. Some fifty-five farmers' co-ops handle 40 per cent of the national egg trade, and increasingly are going into poultry dressing. The consumers often operate egg-grading stations, and CWS has twenty-one depots supplying eggs to retail co-ops.

Fourteen creameries are owned by the Scottish Co-operative Wholesale Society, as well as three large farms and four tomato-growing establishments. One month's milk and creamery business amounts to almost $2,000,000.

A splendid 350-acre dairy farm operated by SCWS is Monktonhill, in Ayrshire. Shortly after its purchase a neighboring farmer said that it was a pity that such a good place had fallen into the hands of the co-operative "to make a mess of." A year later, conceding that it was looking very well, he explained that he had not known that Andrew McBride was to be the manager.

Mr. McBride, head of the SCWS milk department, is responsible for three farms. These are run fairly intensively, as average sales approximating £73 per acre (that's $204) would indicate. Monktonhill is devoted almost entirely to production of milk and pedigree cattle although cash crops of wheat and potatoes are grown to a limited extent. It is largely self-sufficient in feedstuffs, and only bran and a small quantity of protein are bought. One heifer has taken first prize at the Royal Highland show, a feat repeated with variations by co-op farm operations in many parts of England as well.

Monktonhill's herd of Ayrshires includes 100 milk cows and 110 young stock of all ages. Besides breeding all herd replacements, Mr. McBride sells a considerable number of good quality pedigree heifers and bulls.

The type of farming at Blairgowrie, 635 acres in Perthshire, is different. From 22 acres of raspberries there the co-op preserve factory at Shieldhall receives 88 tons. Besides good yields of oats, barley, wheat and stock seed potatoes, the farm grazes 200 cattle and as many sheep.

"All these are sold off, grass fat, in the back end of the year," Mr. McBride explains. "The cattle courts are filled with 150 fresh store cattle in October; these are fed through the winter and are graded during March and April. In the winter we also feed 400 hogs for early spring marketing."

On the 458-acre Aberdeenshire farm there are 180 feeding cattle and 20 pedigree Shorthorn cows with calves at foot, as well as 350 breeding ewes with 600 lambs. Seven hundred turkeys are prepared for the Christmas market, and 700 chickens are kept in the deep litter system. There are 3,000 laying fowls on free range, and 30,000 accredited chicks are hatched, many being sold as day-olds.

The largest retail co-operative in Scotland, St. Cuthbert's, is selling off one large farm holding but is retaining Overshiels farms, 1,500 acres, somewhat nearer its headquarters at Edinburgh. This large operation includes market gardening, pig production, grain and fodder growing and even Percheron horse breeding in addition to dairying. It is stocked with 420 Ayrshires, 900 hogs of the Large White breed, and 400 lambs are fed through the winter. A spotless milking parlor of eight units is the center of dairy operations. Milking is by machine, and the stainless steel fixtures that pipe the milk to the cooler are dismantled twice daily for steam cleaning. Pasteurization is carried on in an adjacent building, and bottling is at six o'clock each morning.

British consumer co-operatives operate more than one-ninth of all dairies, with over one-third of the milk trade. The standard price is about nine cents a pint, more being charged for tuberculin-tested milk. In Cheshire twenty-seven local societies have federated to operate a dairy plant at Hyde costing $840,000, and with a weekly capacity of 160,000 gallons. CWS itself has thirty-six dairies with a yearly output valued at more than $41,000,000.

Such consumer action does not appear to have widened the gap between town and country in England, where so much of the food has to be imported. No further expansion of co-op farming seems likely, though co-op milk distribution may continue to boom. The dairy department of London Co-operative Society added $480,000 to the general dividend for one year. The contrast between this sharing with purchasers and a possible state subsidy for governmental operation at the expense of the taxpayers can hardly be missed.

# [ IV ]

## ECONOMICS IN KILTS

### 1. CHALLENGE AND RESPONSE

THE general manager of the Scottish co-ops' milling department, William Grant, sat in his handsome paneled office at
a desk equipped with push buttons and an intercommunicating
device connecting all parts of Chancelot mills. At a Princes
Street luncheon this same gentleman had told us with pride that
his mother had scrubbed these mill floors when he was a boy. As
mops with handles are not yet familiar to Edinburgh, this was
indeed a labor of love for her fatherless family—down on hands
and knees with soap and water.

There with us was Neil S. Beaton, the grand old man of British
co-operation, himself the son of a shepherd in a remote island
closer to the Arctic Circle than one thinks of Scotland. Before
retiring from the presidency of the Scottish Co-operative Wholesale Society he had made two speaking tours of co-op and labor
groups in the United States. His gentle, restrained manner gives
no hint of his career as a trade union organizer, consumer propagandist and economic statesman. Even in semi-retirement he is
now on three national boards concerned with hydroelectric
power, mines and railroads.

These two Scots are representative of the sort of men who
come to the top through service to the co-ops. Abilities great as
theirs would not have been likely to have found opportunity

otherwise. For in the British world of affairs family and means almost always are required to prime the pump of success.

William Grant, from the time he was old enough to work, attended night classes, nineteen years of them. Doubtless most of his courses were of a technical nature, but somewhere along the line he learned much about people and how they respond to the challenge of responsibility and real opportunity.

Many of the gains of co-operation today are taken for granted, and therefore seem less exciting to the younger generation. Broadening of the educational system now allows gifted boys and girls from every sort of home more opportunities of entering professions with more obvious scope for their talents. The question arises, who is to carry on in the new generation when the spirit of indignation that bred the consumer movement has died? In some commercial ventures as well as in the co-ops there is now a degree of social vision and also the ability to lower distribution costs by integration of factories and shops.

"I don't believe that it is possible to keep the original outlook," Mr. Grant answered. "The spirit of adventure is still very much alive, and the appetite of youth in all times is for a bold offensive, not just to hold what is in their hands.

"It is no use merely prattling to young people so that co-operation ends as merely an empty catchword. We must try to impress them with the inspiring struggles recorded in our early history. Having first caught the imagination, training should turn to economics and the fundamental difference from the ordinary selfish and materialistic approach. It is folly for directors and managers of co-operative societies to preach ideals and at the same time be unable to show everyday examples of what is to be striven for."

Co-ops are people, but the Scots never forget that co-ops are business, too. If it were not for the ability of Scottish character to dream dreams this might seem simply another form of capitalistic enterprise. Most members sign up for their own economic benefit as a means of saving, but at the same time making capital the servant instead of the master. The underlying conviction, however, is that the profit system is in need of thorough overhauling.

The mainspring of co-operative success was pointed out by William Maxwell, president of SCWS in 1888, in these words: "Our co-operative aim must not be to produce or distribute for morbid gain only, but it should be to work together in affection and harmony, so that we may be all morally and physically enriched and purified. Here really is the kernel of co-operation, despite our differences about detail, the point we are all marching on is the brotherhood of man."

Over the tea Mr. Beaton commented that in all great forward movements the crusading spirit enables the pioneers to accept hardship with little hope of reward, He continued: "Later comes a stage, with the first objectives realized, when some crusaders feel that they can relax a little without losing ground. This is the testing time. Only when co-operators lean back with a sense of easy victory will the crusade be at an end."

The dynamic nature of the mill operation is manifest in its personnel policies as well as in its yearly surplus of more than a quarter million dollars. The manager is careful never to ask anything of the force that he is not willing to match. When a Sunday shift is necessary he appears himself, and every morning he comes to work ten minutes before the force.

The telephone switchboard operator at Chancelot is a war veteran with only one lung; he was lifted from despair after his job hunting had seemed hopeless. In the SCWS mill at Glasgow the phones are answered by a member of the British Legion who had walked the streets until his stump of a leg would not heal, just looking for someone to hire him. After medical care he feels useful and secure. Mr. Grant says he would die for the co-op.

"We have felt that the person in charge of the telephones is our direct contact with the outside world, and should have sufficient character and experience to meet all kinds of inquiries tactfully and cheerfully," the manager explained.

"The phone is not for a bairn," Mr. Beaton agreed.

The Chancelot operator's Leith accent being a trifle broad, he was given voice training. With his new hope in life he has broadened his own interests to play the drums in the welfare orchestra, a mill group which entertains old age pensioners, the blind, the ill and otherwise handicapped.

"It takes more than streamlined canteens and brightly painted factories to create a happy atmosphere," Mr. Grant commented. "Co-operation surely means joint effort according to one's capacity. There must never be a suggestion of a benevolent gesture by employers or of humble acquiescence by the employees."

The mills encourage social activities on a self-supporting basis, keeping in mind that no one wants all his leisure organized for him. A dramatic group has been useful in overcoming Scot shyness. There are clubs for bowling, darts and tennis, a summer rambling group, the "Under Twenties" and a students' society to discuss technical problems.

Craftsmen's certificates, with a bonus of thirty dollars, had recently been awarded to eleven flour millers for their knowledge of insect pests, botany and engineering. The tests called for practical performance rather than expression in words that sometimes will not come to manual workers. The course was Mr. Grant's reaction to a BBC radio broadcast to the effect that the spirit of craftsmanship was dying out. He raised the question pointedly at a works meeting.

Later developments led him to apologize publicly to the work force. One of these developments was the gift he received of a polished wood carving, an eight-inch scale model of a wheat grain. Demonstrating this, he removed a portion of the outer husk and layer by layer revealed the construction of the kernel. The man who made it was a joiner in the plant who had studied for several months in the library to get his proportions right.

At the works level joint consultation is encouraged, not merely to exchange gripes but to seek the better and safer way of doing the everyday jobs. What Mr. Grant considers essential is for all these activities to be threaded together with that subtle something described as ideals, in order to make a worth-while whole. His is a humanitarian yet a well-disciplined outlook which considers that society could not exist without mutual aid.

A mill foreman had assigned a former commando to a most monotonous task and, when at length the man rebelled, threatened to fire him.

"You should be sacked, not this lad," Mr. Grant told the boss after an investigation, and found a more stimulating job for the veteran.

Man's relationship to man is the essence of co-operation. Lack of respect for individuality in tastes and interests blocks understanding of common needs. The future, this Scot tells you, is not so much a matter of leadership as of the spontaneous revival of active and widespread interest, the thrill and enthusiasm that comes from worth-while effort.

## 2. LEVELING UP, NOT DOWN

Tradition is that St. Cuthbert's Co-operative Association in its early years selected its directors in alphabetical order from the roll of members. The democratic spirit by now has taken other forms, though the prayer of Robert Browning is still quoted:

> Make no more giants, God,
> But elevate the race at once.

Now more than ninety years old, this Edinburgh co-op is Scotland's largest. It has a membership in excess of 90,000 and a staff of 3,600, of which 600 are in its Bread Street department store. In a guide to new members, Jack Moffatt, the president, notes that the democratic principle applies to employees as well as to members.

"Both have undoubted rights which need to be safeguarded," he writes. "That is to say, the employee must enjoy fair wages and conditions, and the member a right to take part in all deliberations affecting the business."

Out of twenty members of the board of management, four are employees, and there are seven women. All employees are covered by a pension scheme, and, as members, are entitled to free admission to the co-operative convalescent homes in time of need. Staff recreational facilities are provided in a spacious welfare headquarters.

On such occasions as a coronation or the International Festival, horse-drawn landaus make their appearance on the Royal Mile, carrying tourists up to the old castle which dominates the city. These museum pieces are from the rolling stock of St. Cuthbert's, and the horses are bred on its own farm. Among some two hundred modern vehicles operated by the co-op in its business is a fleet of motor coaches for excursion parties and limousines for wedding parties, funeral or other occasions. To provide grocery service for scattered communities sixteen mobile shops daily are pulled to housing developments by what David Shaw, the managing secretary, refers to as "articulated horses." These turn out to be tractors which spot their trailors on strategic shopping sites and pick them up after a day of trading.

In addition St. Cuthbert's operates seventy-five grocery shops throughout the city and suburbs. Many of these are modern self-service establishments, a development that the British co-ops were quick to import from the United States, perhaps as being another form of self-help. There are seventeen drug department branches, an undertaking service and the customary auxiliary tombstone works and florist shops. On death of a member, or the wife or husband of a member, insurance payments up to £50 are available, the size being determined by the yearly purchases—"the greater your purchases the greater the benefit," in the language of the prospectus.

Trading half-years ending in March and September bring forth a twelve-page balance sheet for members. The latest available statement shows sales for twenty-six weeks amounting to £4,484,000 and a dividend of £319,000. This represents a refund to members of 1 shilling 7 pence for each £1 of sales, and to non-members of 9½ pence. The rebate stands just short of 8 per cent on member purchases, exclusive of tobacco and items on which trade restrictions do not permit of any semblance of price reduction.

Share capital is reported at £928,000 and invested capital not required for trading purposes amounts to £759,000, almost half in government securities. Among the investments are sizable shares in the Co-operative Press, in two co-operative clothing factories and in six boot and shoe plants largely owned by the men and women working in them.

The handbook speaks of "a golden opportunity to save," a keynote lately minimized south of the border, where service is being more prominently emphasized. "Members will find it extremely profitable to let accrued dividends remain unlifted as it is automatically added to share capital, on which is paid the high interest rate of 3.5 per cent," the message runs. Recent parliamentary action has raised the limit on holdings of share capital to £500. Interest of 2.5 per cent is paid by a penny savings bank with a limit of £50.

Thrift also motivates the works department, where architects, engineers, electricians, plumbers, painters, masons and blacksmiths are available for repairing homes of members as well as for the maintenance and expansion of the society's holdings.

Also operated by St. Cuthbert's is the Clarendon Hotel, near the Haymarket railway station. This capacious, old-fashioned place is capably managed by Miss Mavis O'Donoghue, and apparently is staffed entirely by young women. It is further remarkable as the only place in the United Kingdom where employees rebuff proffered tips.

"Any kind of food you ask for, I can get it at the co-op," Miss O'Donoghue remarked. When corn on the cob was mentioned, she promptly gave its Gaelic name and went on to say that most cooks boiled the ears too long, toughening the kernels. Even reference to an avocado failed to daunt her confidence.

At dinner that night in the Clarendon a wide-eyed waitress brought in two ears of corn in a soup dish also containing melted butter, and whispered, "Do you eat that in Ameriky?" A few days later on departure I was presented with a green avocado well wrapped in tissue.

"It's not quite ripe," the manageress said, "but take it to Glasgow and open it in the Grand Hotel dining room. They won't even know what it is." This piece of professional jealousy of course was not borne out at the Grand, which is owned by the United Co-operative Baking Society and prides itself on its dining service.

SCWS itself has three hotels, including the Allan Water hotel, a first-class residential place at Bridge of Allan, the Queen's hotel at Perth and the Selborne, at a seaside resort. These reflect the ability of the co-operatives to keep abreast of consumer needs which expand with each generation. When life was largely on a subsistence basis food supply was almost the only co-op service. Now, with paid holidays in business and the consequent increase in travel a CWS subsidiary operates a chain of hotels in coastal resorts around Britain. This same travel agency owns the Ashley Court hotel near Kensington Gardens in London. LCS has its own Ambassadors hotel, and Royal Arsenal Co-operative maintains Shornells in Abbey Wood as a residential center, besides operating two hotels on the Isle of Wight.

More nearly adjusted to the means of the average co-operator is Roseland holiday camp on the Isle of Bute. This was opened shortly after World War I by the United Co-operative Baking Society, on Canada hill, high above Rothesay. Here woodlands and lakes provide opportunities for sport and relaxation. Steamers from Glasgow, forty miles away, bring tired workers from the Clyde shipyards and the coal fields and blast furnaces of Lanarkshire. A family of five in a cottage pays eleven pounds a week in off season and twelve in midsummer, this including meals. This experiment in catering by Scotland's largest baking concern, with its secluded neighborhood of simple wooden chalets across the Clyde from Ayrshire and in view of the majestic hills of Argyll, is quite different from the many noisy and glaring profit-making camps that followed.

Perhaps the brightest jewel in the Scottish co-operative crown consists of the four convalescent homes maintained out of a yearly contribution of two shillings per member by St. Cuthbert's and some 160 other retail societies. The first of these health resorts, Seamill, on the Ayrshire coast, has housed 127,000 patients since its opening in 1896. In a single year more than 8,000 men, women and children are received without any charge in two seaside locations and two others in the Highlands. Their stay customarily is limited to two weeks.

The convalescent home was the first project of the Scottish Co-operative Women's Guild, which financed the beginnings by bazaars and collection of gifts. The desire was expressed to lift the movement to a higher level than "making and dividing profits."

In their opinion [the chronicle reads] the life and soul and glory of the Co-operative Movement consisted in the idea of ameliorating, if it could not wholly remove, the suffering, the misery and the sorrow of the poor struggling masses of the nation; to make the lives of the poorest of the people contented, sweet and happy; and just in proportion as it endeavoured to reach this ideal would the brightness of its fame and honour increase; but in proportion as it set this ideal aside, or delayed in trying to realize it, so would the brightness of its glory and prestige and its claims upon the community decline.

Both SCWS and the baking co-op appropriate £5,000 each year for this amenity which means so much to so many. South from Glasgow, at Largs, is Hollywood home. Originally a luxury tourist hotel, it was requisitioned as an admirality headquarters for Churchill, Mountbatten and Alexander. Then in 1947, with the war ended, it was sold to the co-operatives for £39,000. It is an ideal site, with a distant view across the Firth of Clyde of the hills of Arran and Kintyre. Centering a colorful garden is a ship's mast, reminiscent of its naval connection. Across the main road is the beach and a promenade with deck chairs where patients may sun themselves.

One is struck by the number of frail old women in the spacious, sunlit lounge. A middle-aged man sits at the piano, playing softly as if to himself. A shy boy of seventeen with a heart condition, brought here after an operation by a royal physician, is preparing to leave at the expiration of his two weeks. There are more children at Seamill in West Kilbride; the matron says there are fifteen small girls and boys, the children of sick mothers who felt unable to leave them at home.

In the valley of the Tweed at Galashiels is Abbotsview home, where 2,115 persons, including miners rescued from a pit accident, were cared for in a single year.

The fourth acquisition is Redholm, in North Berwick. This sixty-four-room mansion, which once housed only one family, now accommodates more than 1,000 convalescents annually. The swimming pool has been filled in as a vegetable garden and a greenhouse has been erected.

At each of the homes a gardener divides his attention between the flowers that bloom so colorfully and the tomatoes that bear equally well under glass.

At Hollywood a long battery of laying hens adds its offering to the diet of the guests, a particular blessing in times of rationing and shortage.

The national health service stops short of such facilities for recuperation. Certainly the co-ops have worked out a markedly successful social achievement in providing a change and leisure in which to gain strength after illness. The good done, however, is limited to the families holding membership in the stores. There are those among the most convinced co-operators who say that here is a place where nationalization could assure a benefit to all without weakening the co-ops in any way.

## 3. ACRES OF CO-OPS

Scotland is well advanced along the road of consumer democracy. Co-operative service is available in the most remote communities, even on islands where meager supplies are brought in only by fishing boat. In many localities the co-op hall has become the center of life, for civic affairs as well as for youth groups and men's and women's guilds connected with the movement.

The appeal is to a wider group than in England, including many professional people in addition to the working class. In the

Glasgow area two families out of every three hold membership in one of the seventeen retail co-ops functioning there. The proportions are similar in the mining towns of Lanarkshire, Fife and the Lothians.

The semi-annual dividend on retail purchases long has been a method of automatic saving. In many cases refunds amount to from $21 to $56 each six months. Much of the total is not withdrawn but is left on deposit for some tenaciously held future purpose. One hears of a family that put its four sons through the university on co-op dividends. Jennie Lee, the wife of Aneurin Bevan, herself a Member of Parliament, is said to have received her education by grace of her family's savings at the co-op.

The Scottish dividend is one shilling 6½ pence, a refund of 7½ per cent. Southwest England returns only 7 pence out of each £1 spent. The national average after all allocations is a shilling, or 5 per cent. In 1953 the trading surplus exceeded $122,000,000 after paying share interest.

Possibly there is also more faith in production for use and the elimination of the profit maker as an alternative to traditional forms of business enterprise. Something in addition to domestic thrift is involved in the support given to the idea of the operation of industry in the consumer interest.

A growing multitude seek consciously to replace misery with abundance, ignorance with intelligence, and war, hot, lukewarm or cold, with peace. These are ordinary people, wise only in everyday experience, who realize that if the world is to be transformed it will not be by force but by inner change. If a new social order is to arise, its coming will be gradual, like the blooming of the heather on the Scottish moors. The devastating results of insatiable greed are apparent enough in spite of misleading slogans about what is good for a small minority being good also for the victims of the personal profit system.

"We must replace the capitalist system before disaster," was the way Manager J. Peggie of Leith Provident Co-operative Society expressed this belief. "Economic realities are as sure as the laws of gravity." We were driving through the Highlands with Neil Beaton, who seemed equally proud of the co-operative development and of the success of the North of Scotland Hydro-electric Board, a nationalized power project that is remaking life on the farms and crofts. The talk was of the inability of the economic system to distribute abundance.

"We should produce for ourselves and distribute the same way," Mr. Beaton assented. "We don't want any more capitalists. During the First World War I left trade union organizing when I noticed that increasing prices chased higher wages in ever larger circles. I turned then to promoting co-operatives because I found this the only machinery giving the people direct control of their means of life." Productive capacity in excess of a demand limited by inadequate income seemed to him likely to demoralize employment opportunities.

Some years ago several visiting directors of the Scottish Co-operative Wholesale Society addressed the annual meeting of the Consumers Co-operative Association in Kansas City, Missouri. With no regard for any golden calf, even that bearing the brand of Middle Western farmers, they were outspoken in their criticism of the workings of the capitalistic order.

Not even the tradition of the Populist movement in Kansas or of the Grangers in Iowa had prepared the soil for any such hybrid crop of political and economic wild oats. The Scots' position was that production and consumer distribution should be in the hands of the co-ops; municipal utilities under city ownership, and natural resources, transportation and communication under nationalized operation. In the course of time this neat division of duties has become blurred by attempts to define such co-operative services as milk, bread and coal supply, laundry operation and even undertaking as municipal functions.

In America a co-operative, particularly one with agricultural roots, is a form of free enterprise set up by a group of individuals to perform a service for themselves. The impact has been against the excesses of monopoly and special privilege, not against capitalism as such. Farm movements, even those posing as non-political, have based their demands less on principle and more on expediency. Many a pioneer crusade folded up upon the repeal of discriminatory railroad rates or enactment of state laws against the fraudulent grading of grain.

Aside from any theory, farm purchasing co-operatives in the United States still have a valuable function. And once the spirit of expediency gives way to a realization of the fundamental principles involved, expansion into wider consumer action may be expected.

In Scotland a co-operator may say, "I am a Socialist but—" In America the phrasing is switched to "I am not a Socialist but—" Each refers to the search for a reasonable middle position.

"British co-operation will bear watching," Dr. James P. Warbasse, long the outstanding spokesman of consumer action in the United States, had written me. "It is better, but not yet well of its Socialism. You will find the leaders amazingly good businessmen. They are a great people, and apparently they have given up the notion of making co-operation the tail of the Socialist kite."

Dr. Warbasse credits business sagacity as a quality more likely to be found in co-operation than in public ownership. He ascribes the increase in state functions—"government controlling business and then going into business"—to the failure of profit enterprise to develop a social purpose. To him the world's major problem concerns the method by which the individual will come to subordinate his interests to the general good.

There is a sense of solidarity about the Scottish movement that recognizes, perhaps better than the English, the paramount interest of the people in a satisfactory social adjustment.

The first productive enterprise of the Scottish Co-operative Wholesale Society was a shirt factory, established in 1881 to prove that sweating was not necessary in the needle trades. Later in the same year a tailoring plant was opened. Now SCWS, with headquarters at Glasgow and Edinburgh, has a productive output of more than $80,000,000 a year and a distributive trade just short of a quarter billion dollars. Long famous as one of the first large industrial concentrations is Shieldhall where eighteen SCWS factories have been built on a 116-acre site near the Glasgow docks. Economies from this arrangement include composite loading, and sharing of canteen service, heating, lighting, and building and machinery maintenance.

Not all its plants are at Shieldhall. Tweed is made at Ettrick, paper at Rutherglen, and Taybank jute works is in Dundee. There are flour and oatmeal mills, furniture factories and scattered plants making hosiery, underwear, shoes, hats, waterproof clothing, linoleum, tinware, confectionery, coffee essence, soda water, brushes, soap, preserves, pickles, blankets and many other consumer items. The largest producer and exporter of dried salt fish, SCWS operates fish-curing depots in various ports. Fresh fish are brought from the Aberdeen works to retail shops in insulated vans of the most modern description, made by the co-op motor body and cartwright department at Rutherglen.

Scottish retail co-ops have two different roots. The original growth is that of local societies such as at Kilmarnock. This began with thirteen members ninety years ago, with sales for the first year valued at £510. Membership now having risen to 30,000, sales have reached £3,000,000 per annum. This local development has been financed by members and controlled through their quarterly meetings. As a shareholder in SCWS the society has a voice in all wholesaling and productive operations.

Kilmarnock, as a member of SCWS, has helped establish a centralized co-op chain operating 135 branches in fourteen areas, these without any local control. Mr. Beaton, who fostered this expansion when he was president of the Wholesale, explains that in many isolated localities the poverty of the people made it difficult for them to accumulate capital. Moreover, the opposition of feudal landlords and local merchants made those who most needed co-ops afraid to associate themselves with their establishment.

The situation in some Highland neighborhoods and on the islands differs from that of the industrial belt where the bulk of population lives. This is a strip forty miles wide from Kilmarnock in the west to Dundee and somewhat south of Edinburgh on the east, and includes all the main coal fields, steel works, heavy engineering and shipbuilding. In this industrialized section the historic process was to build a co-operative from nothing by pyramiding the savings, a method now handicapped by new tax exactions.

As a contrast Mr. Beaton exhibits the town square of Aberfeldey, where a merchant desiring to retire sold his holdings to SCWS for £25,000. Now the co-op has a "fleshing shop," otherwise called a butcher's, on one corner and fills another side of the market center with a general store selling everything from groceries to furniture and shoes, with a dining room upstairs. At Pitlochry, center of the Tummel Valley hydro scheme, there is another thriving co-op store and café, also without local direction.

Since 1934 SCWS has provided a funeral undertaking service that by now is far the largest in Britain, having sixty-five locations. A chain of drug shops was established three years later in agreement with local societies whose members share in the dividends. There are more than forty of these drugstores scattered about Scotland. An unsuccessful venture some years in the past was the purchase of 10,000 acres of wheat land in Western Canada. The Manitoba prairie, however, is still dotted with SCWS grain elevators, and a wheat-buying agency is maintained in Winnipeg.

A movement to consolidate the Scottish and English wholesales for all purposes has not made significant headway. The Scots maintain their own banking facilities as well as their separate productive units. Since 1901, however, the two have had a limited federation to plant and blend tea and grow and process coffee, cocoa and chocolate, now a $56,000,000-a-year business. In further collaboration they took control of the Co-operative Insurance Society in 1913. On an international scale they are equal partners with the great Swedish co-operative in the British Luma Co-operative Electric Lamp Society.

Operations of SCWS is vested in a full-time Committee of Management of twelve, including a president and a secretary. They are nominated by member societies in quarterly meetings.

The final vote, by postal ballot, is eliminative until one candidate has a majority over all contesting a seat. Each committeeman serves two years, six being elected each year. Salaries of the president and secretary are limited to a maximum of $3,650 annually, and of a committeeman, to $3,090.

In a year SCWS distributes 57,000 tons of sugar, 5,000 tons of tea, 9,000 tons of butter, 15,000 tons of margarine and 111,000 tons of flour. Its 207 member societies receive a refund of 2 pence per £1 of purchases, this adding to any local savings. The United Co-operative Baking Society, which operates independently, has refunded over $10,000,000 in the last twelve years, more than its entire share capital.

When Mr. Beaton flew to the United States in time of war to address the Congress of the Co-operative League of the U.S.A. at Minneapolis, Minnesota, in 1942, he gave this assurance: "Wherever the co-operative has secured a foothold the standards of the people have risen, there has been created a greater sense of civic responsibility, a higher conception of life and a consciousness of obligation to one's fellows."

Since that time a phenomenal growth of co-operation has occurred.

Economic benefits aside, here is a source of democratic experience, an approach to more mature social relationships, in the community and around the world. Important, too, is the fact that there has never been a "must" in co-operation, self-discipline replacing the imperatives in the relationship of government to people.

### 4. WHAT BELONGS TO CAESAR?

The spirit of local independence and of resistance to a centralized state is far from dead in Scotland. Coolness toward further nationalization is evidenced by John M. Davidson, SCWS president and head of the 1955 Co-operative Congress.

"Government schemes for collective enterprise are subject to one serious drawback," he said in a public address, "namely that owing to political vicissitudes bringing electoral changes, circumstances could arise, both in national and local affairs, which might result in state collectivist enterprise being placed completely under the direction of those opposed in principle."

Denationalization of the steel and road transport industries by the Conservative government has given point to such misgivings. Any co-operative function taken over by political means might similarly be turned back to private ownership of an undesirable or unsocial nature. This was pointed out in 1949 by the Co-operative Union. In actual practice provisions in the nationalized sector for representation of consumers as well as workers fall short of any definition of economic democracy.

Mr. Davidson also made the point that control in co-ops is largely localized. Unlike the setup in state-owned agencies: "Every week of the year some twelve to twenty thousand co-operative members are meeting to discuss matters which concern the efficient supply of consumer needs of one-fourth the population." Where traditions of freedom are held in high esteem, he said, voluntary institutions that have demonstrated their ability to service public needs should be encouraged. He added this parting shot:

"The co-operative movement entirely rejects the view that the voluntary method of co-operative organization of trades and services must ultimately give place to state organizations and is simply a transitional stage."

With its devotion to free speech, the *Co-operative News* published a critical article by P. J. Agnew that spoke of "go-as-you-please voluntaryism" as debilitating. Any future Labour government, he declared, should proceed to centralize the co-ops by giving the national federations close control over the local retail societies.

He recommended that the government should help the movement to take over the distribution of milk as an initial experiment, and added: "In many other instances the transfer of food distribution could be effected with co-operative control." Mr. Agnew, a former sectional board member of the Scottish co-ops, thus would see the movement as an agent of state welfare planning, stopping short of final absorption by the government.

The mounting dilemma is none too comfortable for partisan functionaries such as Andrew Duncan, Scottish national organizer for the Co-operative party. While he has no clear-cut answer to the ancient question of what really belongs to Caesar, his test is utilitarian and pragmatic—that which works out for the greatest good of the greatest number.

No social reform is worth while, in his view, if it does not contribute to the improvement of the quality of the individual. To him the business of government is to plan the economy in such a way as to enable all to do their best. Cartelization, in the guise of trade association control of prices, output and sales practices, makes a sluggish and restrictive economy. He contrasted such private monopolies with a state monopoly which he said frees the individual from the grasp of special privilege.

New and powerful incentives are counted on to arise from any real adjustment between individual objectives and general social conditions. The balance of personal freedom with social justice would encourage men to make larger personal contributions to society.

The whole community would benefit, Mr. Duncan said, from any lifting of commercial toll gates, and some functions can best be carried on by governmental action. He referred particularly to the national health service. It seemed that he had just acquired a new upper denture from the nationalized dental profession, at a personal and direct cost of about six dollars. As set up by the late Labour government there would have been no cost, but Mr. Duncan was in no mood to object to the new Conservative requirement that half of the cost of the raw materials should be borne by the beneficiary.

The position of the Tory government is not in opposition to the basic purposes of health insurance. Though that reform has been removed from political debate, the general question of further extension of public ownership has not. Prime Minister Churchill, whose government passed legislation removing restrictions on co-op financing about which the Labour government did nothing, adroitly seeks to widen differences among his opposition.

"There are now grave doubts about the theory of nationalization and there are even more disagreements about the practice," he said. "The trade unions and co-operatives are organizations in daily contact with reality. They are not hunting for votes and political notoriety but facing facts. There is anxiety among them lest, for the sake of political slogans, the practical interests of the large masses for which they are responsible will be endangered. A few years ago, nationalization was the cure-all for social and economic difficulties; now there is a general feeling that it is a flop."

Divested of all partisan exaggeration, the situation is one in which the British electorate is sitting on its hands, not applauding nationalized coal, electricity or railroads, nor acclaiming the return of the steel industry to cartelized operation.

Where British industries have been nationalized it is not for socialism's sake. Subsidies had been necessary for the coal mines and railways before their taking over, and compensation for the former owners represented something other than confiscation. The high cost of indemnifying private ownership in any gradual, democratic change to public operation has encouraged the idea that controls and central planning might achieve the same ends at less cost.

From time to time isolated co-operative societies balk at support of the Co-operative party machinery. Four out of fourteen Scottish co-ops in the Falkirk area have voted against political action of any kind, and to refuse to authorize the customary halfpence-per-member deduction for political purposes. In vain has Mr. Duncan appealed to their pride in the Co-operative contingent in Parliament. He called attention to the large experience in trade, manufacture and democratic practices which fitted co-operators particularly to carry out state ownership as well as to establish a co-operative commonwealth. Even references to the importance of local political responsibilities failed to develop any enthusiasm.

In many communities local councils now are controlled by
Labour party majorities. These frequently have leaned over backward in attempting to assure the electorate that they are not
giving any special favors to the co-ops. In the case of public
housing developments, where store rooms are to be assigned or
leased to grocers and other merchants, the co-operatives have
run into obstacles. In many instances their own members have
moved from the slums to new council housing, yet it may be
that they can be served only through a rolling grocery, a butcher
shop on wheels and a traveling dry goods store.

This matter of local political relations is one of great concern
to the entire co-operative movement, which basically is skeptical
of political centralization, and also apprehensive of duplication of
its services at the expense of the taxpayers.

In effect the Co-operative party's Scottish Committee of Local
Government has advised municipalities to take over the profitable
branches of public recreation instead of using tax funds for only
those out of which no profit could be made. As a saving to rate
payers and not an additional burden, it does not even neglect
civic operation of indoor and outdoor dancing.

"Local authorities at the moment let their halls—sometimes at
a loss—to dance bands and others, allowing them to pick up the
profit," the report points out. Sports stadiums for greyhound and
dirt track racing, football and other contests "could be operated
under the local authority, also sports events organized." Exhibi-
tion centers in the larger cities would house musical and dramatic
entertainments and encourage such organizations as Citizens
Theater and the Scottish Orchestra.

The final listings include "Provision and operation of ceme-
teries, crematoria, abattoirs and slaughter houses where required, and public markets for fruit, meat and fish, but not the
wholesaling of these commodities." Civic restaurants, school
meal service and catering facilities for public events are also suggested, as is a mutual insurance system for public buildings on an
area basis.

This plainly is no millennium, but it is designed to give Labour party councilors on the local level some other target than the taking over of co-operative dairies or bakeries.

The problems of local government also have been under the study of the National Committee of the Co-operative party, which has been alarmed by the shift of power from the localities to the center in Whitehall. The committee report suggests a new partnership between central and local government to be worked out on a basis of mutual responsibility and respect.

As one means of giving local government a more dynamic role the co-operators suggest experimenting with local town meetings to discuss matters of community interest and explain policies. Another means of contact is seen in closer official relations with parent-teacher associations.

"We are concerned about local government because it is a precious heritage which is now threatened not by its own inherent faults, but by our failure to adapt it to the changing needs of our time," the report continues. It reasons that the family is so important to a person's self-respect and self-development because one is made to feel important in his own right.

The problems of apathy in any society can be tackled constructively only when that lesson is learned [the reasoning goes]. Here is the case for the neighborhood council, a meeting of representatives of the neighborhood unit in urban areas—where the problem of finding personal significance is perhaps most acute—in which certain limited responsibilities could be vested. They would be responsibilities in which the interest is wholly or mainly with the small community living within the neighborhood unit. All this implies that we should seek to relate the interest, understanding and experience of the largest possible number to the problems of the community, for in that time-worn definition of democracy it is "government by the people" which makes it distinctive.

This fundamental respect for the individual's importance is one of the reasons why, in spite of the principle of open membership, co-operatives have not suffered from Communist infiltration. There is little evidence of a Communist clique manifesting itself, or even of individual Communists exercising any great influence.

Faith in the democratic process is strong enough to burst any bonds of class consciousness. Moreover, as a form of social action, co-operation is the expression of a philosophy of life, its quality of moderation needed in any economic and political climate.

A strong line has been taken by the International Co-operative Alliance in a resolution demanding for the movement "freedom of activity on the basis of its own principles." In repelling efforts for political control the resolution closes with this statement: "That the co-operative movement, wherever a regulated economy in some form or other has been put in power, rejects measures that hinder the national or international development of its activity, just as it rejects any efforts in a socialist economic state to concentrate the whole economic activity in the hands of public bodies."

# [ V ]

# GUIDES TO THE FUTURE

## 1. Happy Hoedown

A NOTED London editor remembers with gratitude that his
first knowledge of poetry and music came from participation in a children's choir conducted by a co-op in the slums of Glasgow. Such choral groups, like the orchestras and dramatic societies similarly sponsored, do much to bring light and color into young lives. And in lifting their spirits above the sometimes drab surroundings a further gain is found—the pleasure and satisfaction that come from merging individual effort for some joint accomplishment.

In such small ways may the growth of personality begin, bringing new sets of values and habits that redound to the benefit of a group. And so youth work holds high priority in many co-operatives, undoing as far as possible the individualistic effects of traditional school methods. The feeling that formal education and post-school environment tend to ruin the qualities making for co-operation prevails.

"If we can succeed in thinking of one another in terms of true friendship, without wanting to assimilate, amputate or destroy one another, then we shall become co-operators," the 18th Congress of the Co-operative Alliance was told by the noted Swiss spokesman, Ch.-H. Barbier. "The press, the radio, the cinema, with their colossal influence and their almost limitless resources, are mediums which have only passive appeal, which create passivity, which spread and nurture it. It is passivity which is most often engendered in the child by the education of its parents; and the ignorance of so many mothers, who do not know better than to act for the child in the most simple things which concern it, kills the child's need to act for itself. Again, traditional teaching methods by which the instructive activity of the master takes the place of the laborious work of the child develops passivity in the schoolboy."

His resolution against egocentric training of the young and calling for more dynamic educational methods was unanimously adopted by ICA.

As a counteractive to social apathy a wide range of activities is carried on by the co-operative youth movement in three age groups from seven to twenty-one years. The International Federation of Young Co-operators, formed in 1953, seeks to influence youth everywhere to take their place as responsible citizens in a democratic community. The approach is through pleasurable activity designed for character building.

One of the advantages of the ready-money position of the co-operatives is their ability to buy some fine old country estates, useless to the family heirs but invaluable for group purposes. Stanford Hall, the Co-operative College four miles from Loughborough, is a fabulous country place with a private theater to which the former owner would bring his guests by the trainload from London. As taken over by the Co-operative Union, it has added an ample library to classroom and dormitory facilities and the old bowling green, cricket pitch, putting green and outdoor swimming pool.

In a different category are three youth centers operated for holidays with a purpose. Dalston Hall, a fifteenth-century castle on the Scottish border, is one of these. Many weekend schools as well as week-long outings make use of this 115-acre estate three miles out of Carlisle. Another center is Collington Rise at Bexhill-on-Sea in Sussex, and the newest is Losehill Hall, Castleton, in Derbyshire.

For a brief time in lovely surroundings even the sons and

daughters from crowded slums are enabled to live as they should like. It is an emotional experience to see these girls descend Dalston Hall's grand marble staircase, moving graciously but as if in a dream come true. Even tough little boys from the Liverpool docks respond to this new environment, not out of regard for its splendor from the past but for its opportunities to participate as a team in a constant round of activities.

The culminating entertainment of one week at Dalston Hall was a night of German singing and dancing, girls in dirndls and boys in shorts, with felt hats reblocked in Alpine shape and even with home-made alpenstocks. No trouble to interest these children in such a venture into international empathy. It was not a performance, there was no stage, and parents who came to watch sat with the dancers at their tables.

Another successful entertainment which required extensive planning by its participants was advertised in posters as "Happy Hoedown on an American Farm." The setting was fairly easy, after the fashion of *Oklahoma!* The words and music of authentic farm songs were found in a booklet published by the United States Department of Agriculture, and a set of barn dance records was borrowed from the American embassy. These English boys in their checked shirts and neckerchiefs and the girls in billowing square dance skirts were too busy having a good time to feel that they were showing off. The children were entertaining themselves, from the drawing of the first poster and cutting out a cardboard chicken for the henhouse to the last call of "Promenade all."

These adolescents from the cities at first find the quiet of the country night strange and are slow to quiet down for sleep. Once the spirit of team play takes hold, however, life runs in smooth channels. Not penalties, but rewards are depended upon to bring out social attitudes. Each team for one summer period had its own totem pole, on which credits were registered for actions showing consideration for others. Even such small attention as a boy holding a door open to let girls pass first is noted by an instructor and the merit assigned to his team.

This is different from the old method which put a premium on the memorizing of historical facts such as "Co-operation began in 1844 at Rochdale."

"What good is knowledge if children haven't learned to settle their own squabbles intelligently?" asks G. D. Dust, sectional education officer for the Co-operative Union.

The effort is for effective exercises in practical democracy, involving many compromises between the individual and the group, and social experiences giving confidence and training for community life.

Youth club leaders are using an American film to encourage voluntary group efforts in the schools and wherever young people meet. This is *Skokie School Store—a Consumers' Co-operative*. The script describes how junior high school students of the Chicago suburb of Winnetka apply Rochdale principles. A co-operative school store handles a great variety of supplies, does wholesale buying, works out sales prices, builds up working capital and makes regular distribution of savings to members. A credit union also is run by these boys and girls, making short-time loans from savings desposits. There is even a mutual insurance enterprise established by the student council to cover breakage of dishes in the school lunchroom.

It is through such practice as well as precept that the common purposes necessary to the preservation or development of modern civilization are encouraged. Instead of the predatory, egocentric impulses which Mr. Barbier and the ICA fear, a sense of solidarity, a reconciliation of private interests with the general good, is set in motion.

At all age levels from the Playway groups (seven to ten years) through the Pathfinders (eleven to fourteen) and Co-operative Youth Clubs (fourteen to twenty) the aim is to develop character, allowing the child to find himself in service to others of his own age.

An outdoor group not directly associated with the Co-operative Union but supported by many local societies is the Wood-craft Folk. Its program of weekend hiking and summer camps involves the Elfins (seven to ten years old) and the Pioneers (ten to fifteen). Weekly meetings include folk dancing, singing, dramatics, games, craft work, talks and discussions. The overall purpose as signed by new members reads as follows:

I declare that I will do my utmost;
To camp out and keep fit in mind and body,
To work for world peace and co-operation,
To understand the mysteries of nature and the history of the world so that I may take my place as an intelligent and useful member of Mankind.

International understanding is one of the main goals of the whole co-operative youth movement, particularly of the British Federation of Young Co-operators, which covers the twenty-one-to-twenty-eight-year age group. Student exchanges and club trips abroad supplement general courses on European co-operation. The magazine, *Young Co-operator*, makes much of leadership training and of gains made through attendance at a meeting of the International Federation of Young Co-operators held in Germany. New domestic interests have been opened up by weekend schools on "Design in Our Homes" in preparation of leaders for winter programs on matters of good quality and design in housing, furniture and household equipment generally.

Under co-operative auspices also are some one hundred dramatic groups. Importance is attached to the little theater in the conviction that the arts have much to teach men and women in thinking through the problems of social democracy. The dramatist often is the leader of progressive thought, a fact noted by the education committee of the Newcastle upon Tyne Society which makes no secret of its desire to influence thought and opinion through the stage.

In Nottingham voluntary workers transformed an old chapel into a co-op art center. There professional producers train dramatic, choral and orchestral organizations. Vaughan Williams, a noted composer, has praised its presentation of his opera, *Hugh the Drover*, as the best in his experience.

The Arcade Players at Long Eaton have offered Shaw's *The Doctor's Dilemma*, but in the main strike a lighter note such as in Philip King's *Without the Prince* and *Young Wives' Tale* by Ronald Jeans. The amateur operatic section of the society's senior choir concentrates on Gilbert and Sullivan, a recent production being *The Yeoman of the Guard*.

Cognizant of the lack of modern material, the Co-operative Union is offering to purchase plays, either of one act or of three or more, with the British Drama League judging the offerings. The stipulation reads: "It is particularly desired that the highest artistic standards should be maintained, and whilst plays for the serious discussion of ideas will be welcome, those of a narrow propagandist type are neither sought nor desired."

Ruskin in his *Fors Clavigera* spoke of the co-operative stores as "a good and wise beginning, no less." Through the years their basic social philosophy has opened the windows of the mind for all those who have been touched by understanding. The soul itself has been freed and unsuspected capacities discovered and set to work as in a vision. This younger generation, not using education as a trap door to escape from responsibility, can bring the good life closer to realization.

## 2. IMPORTANT ROLES FOR WOMEN

When Howard A. Cowden, head of the Consumers Co-operative Association, itself a wholesale and production agency serving 1,600 American co-ops, visited England a few years ago he remarked that he would like to see about two hundred capable British Guildswomen transplanted to the Middle West. To appreciate the cogency of his statement one must know something of CCA as well as of the Women's Co-operative Guild.

CCA, with headquarters in Kansas City, Missouri, has spread to ten states, from Wyoming to Iowa, since its founding in 1929. Local member co-operatives serve approximately 456,000 patrons, of whom about 98 per cent are farmers. With two subsidiaries it processes and supplies practically all the gasoline, oil, feed, fertilizer, lumber and paint for the retail societies. Only in the food trade has it been unable to make progress, first selling off its large cannery and then discontinuing grocery wholesaling. The successful operator of four oil refineries, with a business of $57,-000,000 in petroleum products for one year, it could not find support for a kitchen commissary department.

In such matters of domestic supply the housewives rule. "The Woman with the Basket," to use the phrasing of a deeply moving book by Catherine Webb, is necessary for the success of any consumer movement. In the British co-ops the part played by women is steadily widening. A compilation by the Scottish Guild shows 117 of its members on boards of management, 192 on educational committees, as well as a representation of one each in the National Committee of the Co-operative party, the United Baking Society and the Co-operative Union.

From its beginning some seventy years ago the Women's Co-operative Guild has been a training ground, first in self-education and later for civic responsibilities. That same Scottish poll found 14 Guildswomen on town or county councils and 32 as justices of the peace. Seven English Guildswomen are mayors and 15 others are the wives of mayors.

It does not do to forget that consumer co-operation was born and reared through unrest and that its early history was one of agitation. The vigor and directness of Pioneer days, surviving in the Guild movement, is not always pleasing to a business management that desires to be left alone. The Guild slogan in a current campaign, "Lower prices and lower dividends," is capable not only of remaking co-operative policy but also of narrowing margins and increasing efficiency in the distributive field.

Many times these earnest and conscientious housewives have been a thorn in the flesh of the more conservative menfolk. Their advocacy of equal suffrage was not surprising in view of their having held voting membership in their local societies for many years. But when they went further, to advocate relaxation of the rigid divorce laws, the Co-operative Union for a time canceled their subsidy.

In its meager beginnings consumer co-operation tended unthinkingly to adopt the low labor standards of the day. Credit for awakening the conscience of the movement, ending the sweating of women in co-op employment and setting a minimum wage goes to the Guild. First a roll of honor was established for shops meeting the higher standards, and later the shorter work week was pioneered. Practically every co-op employee is a trade unionist, and wage scales for the 350,000 men and women workers are above the general level, with benefits including contributory pensions and sickness, maternity and vacation leave.

"Many of the social services which are in operation today and so casually accepted by the general public whenever they are needed were brought about by the hard work and persistence of the Guilds through the years," says Mrs. Florence M. Cornillie, vice-chairman of the million-member London Co-operative Society. "In spite of tremendous opposition, maternity and child welfare clinics, state medical service, nursery schools, meals for school children, increased old age pensions and divorce law reforms have been brought about, always with Guild backing."

Mrs. Cornillie sits on the LCS board of management, of which half the members are housewives. She mentions the long and successful struggle to win acceptance for women for positions once considered the sole right of men, as members of Parliament, as magistrates and in the professions. The next drive is toward equal pay for equal work, or the "rate for the job," as she calls it.

"We realize that this is a very difficult question," Mrs. Cornillie admits, "as in many cases it is not too easy to show that women are actually doing the work of men, but there are many jobs that women are doing equally well with men. And here we say that by act of Parliament it should be obligatory on all employers, not only the co-ops, to give women a square deal."

Accepting an invitation to visit Soviet Russia's co-operatives, five members of the Guild subjected themselves to considerable criticism for their reports from behind the iron curtain. Women, they wrote, appear to hold most senior positions in the Russian co-operative movement. Mrs. Mabel Ridealgh, general secretary of the English Guild, and herself a former Member of Parliament, was impressed by the tremendous progress made by Russian women in public positions. The visitors found no co-operative shops in Moscow, these having been replaced by state stores, so they went to a nearby village to see some. Prices seemed high but people were buying. Mrs. Ridealgh considered some of the things they saw a little out of date, and compared the adding machines to children's bead boards.

International understanding and world peace are encouraged by contacts between guildswomen of many nations. The co-operative movement remains one of the few groups preserving membership on both sides of the East-West divide. The Scottish Guild opens its meetings with this anthem:

> Round the world a new song's ringing,
> Listen, women of all climes—
> 'Tis the mothers' song we're singing,
> Telling hopes of happier times:
> We will put all hate behind us—
> We whose hearts are sick and sore,
> Tired of strife and empty vict'ries,
> Bear the pangs of war no more.

These wives and mothers sing on:

> For our eyes have seen the vision
> Of a world where peace doth reign,
> Linked in one co-operation—
> Peace o'er all our final goal!

The exchange of visits with Swedish women has encouraged the demand for more confidential relations between British housewives and CWS. The Scandinavian co-operative establishment has made much of women's advisory and testing committees. Before any new piece of household equipment is put on the market, the opinion of the women who are to buy it and use it is obtained. Only a beginning of this relationship has been made in Britain, the approach being through the CWS market research department. However, testing panels drawn from three hundred Guild members in the Manchester district have helped to settle such questions as the best color for Spel detergent, whether it should be perfumed and what the right amount of lather should be.

"The co-operative movement is essentially a woman's movement," said a Guild speaker at Cardiff, calling for more say in the running of societies. "We are the people who can instill into the minds of our officials what is needed by the members."

In the matter of clothing manufacture it appears from the slow expansion of sales that not enough attention has been paid to the desires of women shoppers. A resolution adopted unanimously by the Scottish Guild reads:

> That this Congress of Scottish Co-operative Guildswomen would once more remind the SCWS directors of a previous request for the establishment of a Consultative Committee from chosen Guild representatives—not on technical lines but as organized consumers. The Guilds are at all times willing to co-operate with their societies and with the SCWS to give advice based upon practical experience and a firm belief in the Co-operative Movement.

The demand for consultative councils is backed by the general secretary of the English Guild, who adds a call for specialist shops to cut overhead charges and provide expert advice for shoppers.

In the co-op beginnings the demand was for hard-wearing goods representing economy and ignoring anything resembling a display of style. With the new generation, however, there are different standards. So, when the time arrives that daughter Mary becomes fashion-conscious, it's, "Oh, Mom, not at the Stores!"

The great gains in sales of women's dress have been made by chains of specialty shops and bazaars that neglect outsize customers to furnish attractive apparel for the young and slender. With the spread of middle age, Mary will find her way back to the co-op stores but in the meantime this department languishes.

Failure to obtain mass production, partly due to the proclivity of local co-ops to order minor alterations in otherwise standard coats and dresses, has its effect on margins and prices. To a degree the choking of the supply line springs from the otherwise praise-worthy desire to be good employers. Promotion as buyers or department managers is generally on lines of seniority, co-op employment in many ways resembling the security of civil service.

"Jack's been with us for twenty years," is enough to guarantee a managerial promotion. Particularly in the smaller co-ops this may result in stocks of conservative pattern, harking back to the union flannel age. The colorful and showy chains never know such a crisis as this, but then, neither can they find the loyal service that comes from providing job security.

Politically the Guilds are active in the effort to turn out the Tory government, particularly on the issue of the rising cost of living. Petitions to Parliament have objected to the rapid removal of rationing and price controls. Some Guilds are seeking to draw in younger members with a broadened program including discussions of nutrition, child psychology and home beautification. Though many local leaders resist any idea of changing with the times, two branches have proposed an inquiry into the need for reorganization and reorientation.

Those who have seen the dingy meeting rooms of the Guilds, the dun-colored walls with the black line waist high, the kitchen chairs and the infirm teacups will rejoice that in London at least these halls are being redecorated with pastel shades and bright canvas tubular chairs, even though carpets are still lacking.

Coincidentally a reading course based on Margaret Llewellyn's booklet *Design in Our Homes* has been recommended by the Co-operative Union. This stresses the important part the co-ops should play, as a movement of social aims, in releasing people from "dreary, unsatisfying and inefficient conditions of living." To quote directly:

Some would mock the suggestion, but I would argue that the people of this country have long been starved of the enjoyment of beauty—so long that they may not know a beautiful thing when they see it. . . . But the capacity for enjoyment is there, and to develop that appreciation is to add delight to living. . . . We certainly should accept such a responsibility, not because it is desirable in some abstract way, and not only because appreciation of design carries economic advantages, but because it means, literally, more fun for more people. The beauty of good design (and of literature, art and music) is not merely the "icing on the cake"; it is part of that fuller life for all the people to which our political and social activities are devoted.

### 3. School of Democracy

Co-operative living calls for a process of re-education, both cultural and vocational. The problem of the consumer movement lies less in how to expand its trade than in how to give its members a lively sense of participation in social change.

The Co-op is a shop and a symbol of civilization [a statement drawn up for the Festival of Britain in 1951 began]. In other shops the customers buy from the proprietors, but in the Co-op the customers ARE the proprietors. The whole Co-operative Movement is an association of partners in mutual trade—partners who buy for themselves, sell to themselves and share the benefits. Slowly and surely these Co-op members are shaping a new form of society in which ordinary men and women manage their own business affairs and organize their own social and cultural activities.

Shock troops of the co-operative advance are groups of men and women who may occupy no official positions but are free to scrutinize operations from inside the movement in a critical but constructive manner. Later in origin than the Women's Guild are two similar organizations providing for service by men as well as women, schools for aggressive leadership. One of these is a product of the new age in which husbands and wives find pleasure in going out together, the National Guild of Co-operators. This now is negotiating for amalgamation with the National Co-operative Men's Guild, which was established in 1911. No such consolidation of effort has any attraction for the Women's Guild, jealous of its outstanding position as a sort of housewives' trade union. However, all have as their primary object the arousing, maintaining and increasing of interest in the workings and development of the movement. As expressed by the men's group but common to all the general aim is to "make known the principles of co-operation and assist toward their universal application to human affairs."

In an early number of the *Guildman* magazine, N. H. Gregory, now a director of the Co-operative Wholesale Society, wrote that experience had shown that many a man would listen to an address over a friendly pipe, or come to a debate with his fellow co-operators at a Guild branch, who would not go to a class or even to one of those propaganda concerts where a lecture is sandwiched between musical numbers. With the increasing size of business operations he saw danger of a gulf developing between those conducting operations and a silent, apathetic multitude. Going further, he noted also the tendency for boards of management to become isolated, not knowing what the general membership is thinking, and unable to understand why sales of certain lines may be falling. Here again, the Guilds seek to act as liaison with directors by undertaking rough-and-ready consumer research.

The Men's Guild, by advocating a policy of low competitive prices and less dividends, is running counter to the general practice of most British co-ops, which observe the current market prices, postponing any saving for consumers until the end of the fiscal period. Co-op consumers have never been educated to know quality, which they tend to judge by price. Uninformed co-operators before this have tended to infer that low prices indicate inferior products. Particularly was this noticeable when CWS began to manufacture soap. Prices at retail, based on production costs, were so low as to discourage any notion of quality. It was not until the original cut prices had been modified upward that members in large numbers would accept brands of their own manufacture.

Now, however, the national president of the Women's Guild has announced support of the campaign for more immediately competitive prices as a step toward a general reduction of living costs. This fits in with the women's vigorous crusade in defense of food subsidies and against removal of price controls by the Conservative government.

Such action programs represent an advance in co-operative thinking, the blossoming of a long process of education set in motion by the Rochdale Pioneers. In the days before the Friendly Societies Act authorized deductions from earnings for educational purposes, the Rochdalers opened a reading room and library, in addition to classes for children. When it could be done legally, the Pioneers allotted 2.5 per cent of the trading surplus to education. This now has been halved at Rochdale, and the practice is neglected in some societies. In the larger groups, however, a separately elected educational committee, usually with a paid secretary, conducts cultural and vocational programs.

The overall purpose of strengthening democracy is stressed by the National Co-operative Education Association. A woman delegate from Bristol told a convention of this group that members should understand that the primary aim of the co-op movement was to bring about a new social order, and obtained unanimous approval of a resolution for adequate grants.

A spokesman for the Co-operative Press at the same meeting expressed the feeling that the chief activity of every nation was directed, not to improving the life of the people, but to inventing more destructive means for wiping out whole peoples. "Unless we can bring to our educational work a keener appreciation of the real purpose of life, we shall have failed," he said.

Shortsighted desire for larger dividends and fewer deductions has resulted in curtailment of some co-operative cultural effort, usually with the excuse that school facilities are adequately provided by local authorities. To a certain extent this is true in vocational training, but there can be no substitute for such co-op functions as the character-building policy of the youth movement. Now that educational opportunities are less restricted, a happy relationship has developed in which local governments make available technical courses of use to co-op employees. There are, furthermore, national grants for adult education, and in many cities a department of further education offers the services of lecturers whose topics range from introductory talks on philosophical, economic or scientific subjects to homecraft and musical appreciation.

In the Glasgow area seventeen federated co-ops offer panel discussions for Guilds and party branches, the subjects ranging from mutual aid on an international basis to the history and aims of the Co-operative party. Some co-ops own movie theaters, and many others foster film societies, some for adults, others for children's Saturday showings. At Rochdale there are still a children's dancing class and a junior choir, and even a rental service for microscopes, binoculars and telescopes.

The first of a now extensive system of tutorial classes was sponsored by Rochdale in 1906, enabling university lecturers to reach the minds of working class men and women in a new approach to adult learning. In addition to these university extension courses, retail societies offer hundreds of illustrated lectures on such subjects as *The Need for Planning, Parliament Past and Present* and *Battle Against Poverty*.

The center of formal education is Co-operative College at Stanford Hall, though it stresses technical training rather than general member education. By arrangement its courses on co-operative subjects are credited toward a diploma in social science by Nottingham University. Scholarships awarded by the Co-operative Union and some local societies enable children of members to reach Stanford Hall or go on to Oxford. Balliol College by arrangement with the Union offers a special course at Oxford. On invitation of Bangor Normal College in North Wales, the Union conducts classes for members of education committees and for special students in social science as well as for co-operators interested in dramatic productions. A series of lectures on the co-operative contribution to modern thought extends a particular invitation to students from overseas.

About one-fifth of the Co-operative College enrollment is from other lands, attending through the financial support of the students' government or of colonial or other regional co-op agencies. Of twenty-one from overseas in a single year, four came from India, five from the Gold Coast, two from Tanganyika, Sudan and Trinidad, and one each from Ceylon, Cyprus, Nigeria, Malaya, Sarawak and Surinam. In addition to formal instruction, the benefits of the close contacts of a residential center such as this for persons of diverse background and races are unmistakable. The large country mansion with its three hundred acres of woodland and pasture, a haven of friendship outside the distractions of city life, has become a world center.

Except that the capacious stables of Stanford Hall have been converted into offices for the tutors, and in the main hall the bedrooms cut down into student cubicles, not much has been changed since the days of the former owner, Sir Julian Cahn. In the lovely rose garden bronze statues still crouch among the bordering hedge, a fountain splashes among the water lilies and even the formal Italian garden blooms between blue tile walks. The tennis courts, playing fields and the theater find more use than ever before.

One of the main departments of the College awards a diploma in management, and another gives training in office administration such as is needed for a secretaryship of a retail society. A course in colonial co-operation includes tours of the outstanding co-op developments in the United Kingdom. Extension courses by mail are offered to those unable to leave their home or job. In charge as principal is Col. R. L. Marshall, O.B.E., M.A., chief education officer of the Co-operative Union.

For busy co-operative officials, including management committeemen, and leaders of youth work and discussion groups there are occasional six-day intensive sessions, and even weekend courses. In a slack business season 50 co-op branch managers attended one week's course at Stanford Hall. At the same time one of a series of sessions for outstanding young employees brought 31 more to the school, which has dormitory accommodations for 110 men and women. The summer management studies opened with a lecture on the origin, purpose and development of co-ops, continued with discussions comparing the branch stores with competitors, then turned to such details as window displays and shop practice.

Outside and beyond these college offerings there is a continuous local process of training for both men and women employees. At times it is a demonstration by an experienced butchery manager on how to slice bacon to avoid waste and at the same time to provide a cheaper section for members rationed by their purse. Increasing attention is being given to what is termed "spoken salesmanship" or "member satisfaction." Using the technique of the psychodrama, the instructor dons a white coat and a trainee approaches him as a customer. Later the roles are reversed. Movies are used, as in a study of the physiological elements in fitting shoes or corsets. As a result the employee has more interest and greater satisfaction in his work, the consumer is better satisfied and the society benefits through increased trade.

Many societies offer to pay half the cost of textbooks as well as the major cost of tuition for employees in special classes or correspondence courses. Those showing real capacity and enthusiasm may be sent to the Co-operative College for a year's technical study. Young employees of the London Society are given a booklet which points out their opportunities thus:

If you have the desire and the will to improve your position, there is scarcely any limit to the opportunities ahead of you. It is the policy of the Committee of Management, as far as possible, to fill the higher posts from the ranks of our own staff. The present general manager started with the society as a boy; the present secretary started as an office junior and most of the other leading positions in the society are filled by men with a similar background who have qualified by hard work and loyal service for the positions they now occupy.

The growth of the movement has made it imperative that more members of the staff should expand their theoretical and technical knowledge to supplement their practical experience. At the same time the influx of bright boys into shop employment has been delayed and even diminished by the late Labour administration's extension of the school-leaving age from thirteen years to fifteen. Possibly the caliber of young people drawn into co-op employment is going down as so many able boys and girls find opportunity in higher education.

As yet the co-ops have made no provision for the employment of university graduates such as are recruited into other forms of enterprise. There are no high monetary inducements for special abilities, dependence being placed instead on a sacrificial spirit of service that at times wears thin.

### 4. Purposeful Social Change

The larger co-operatives become, the more important is the orientation of their members. Mere possession of large modern shopping centers does not guarantee the arrival of a consumer economy in a free society. To the extent that business enterprises are able to play on the susceptibilities of an unsophisticated buying public the economics of boom and bust will continue to rule. Skill in making consumers desire goods that are not necessarily beneficial but may be only more profitable to industry offers no substantial foundation for business stability.

There comes a time when producers overestimate their ability to sell goods, and when merchants having built up speculative inventories are left without sufficient demand. Workers are laid off and in consequence become poorer customers until the depression runs its weary course.

The tendency of co-operative economy, on the other hand, is to adjust production to long-term rather than short-term demand, and to hold down prices rather than bid them up. The contrast with profit enterprise is unmistakable.

High pressure marketing methods and advertising, working upon the desire to keep up with the Joneses and the fear of becoming socially unacceptable, attempt to use the powers of psychology to part consumers from their money. Importance is imparted to superficial matters until it not only influences our impulses and desires but further tends to remold human character, a function normally left to education and religion.

Herein lies the importance of general member education such as is carried on by James Leonard, education secretary of South

Suburban Co-operative Society. Many physical advantages have sprung from the amalgamation of smaller co-ops into SSCS, the fourth largest in Britain with its membership of 233,000 in the London area. Benefits of mass distribution are apparent but still the danger exists that social values may be lost to sight in pursuit of economic gains.

Essential to healthy progress, Mr. Leonard will tell you, is a socialized attitude of mind. Great strides have been taken toward a world full of physical satisfactions but the minds and hearts of the people are not sufficiently nourished, he says, to make the most of them. How to assure the co-existence of security and freedom, how to safeguard the individuality and dignity of man, these are the problems of a highly organized society.

His educational aim is to inculcate a sense of responsibility rather than of passive acceptance. A target is set up for each active member to reach and inspire the interest of one apathetic member each year for five years. He put his reasons thus: "For many years before the war, the ordinary citizen was beginning to get used to a new idea, suggested by advertising and commercial interests, that it was his right to receive service from others. The view that it was equally necessary for every individual to give some service to the community has since come to be more and more disregarded. During the war, service to the nation was a statutory decree and did not depend on the opinion of individual citizens. Now the development of the social service state has tended to encourage the citizen to believe that he has a right to service from the state. The necessity for the citizen himself to give service in return is beginning to be quite foreign to the rising generation."

Co-operation can advance no faster than the re-education of man, Mr. Leonard believes. His is a three-fold task, with youth clubs, adult membership activities and staff training, this last in conjunction with the business management. To these duties he brings an unusually broad experience for a man still young—he has been a traveling salesman, free-lance commercial photographer, journalist, dress designer, cosmetic factory manager, television researcher and electronic engineer. Academically he holds the University of London's diploma in social studies.

The function of the co-op educational establishment is to make sure that the cash nexus does not substitute for the active participation and the voluntary spirit that marked the beginning years. South Suburban, with its headquarters in Croydon, has opened one hundred new shops in five years and it averages more than three hundred new members each week. While the incentive to join may be a simple desire for pecuniary advantage or some other benefit, there is still the possibility of a desire to participate coming from a particular social attitude. This is the spark that the co-operative educator strives to fan into a blaze.

Co-operation implies social betterment in proportion to the sum of individual contributions. In education for a consumers' world of mutual aid, what becomes of the competitive spirit? If competition is effective in assuring the survival of the fittest, Mr. Leonard observes, it results eventually in monopoly. To prevent such a development state regulation may be called upon as part of a socializing process, or its alternative, the co-operative way.

One drawback in a system of competition is the eliminative process at each stage of which only the successful can move forward. The winner, establishing a vested interest, must defend it against any new challenge.

"In a monopoly one privileged individual or group is established at the head of a pyramid of subordinates," Mr. Leonard reasons. "In a socialized system there is a restricted area of individual competition within participating groups, for the necessarily limited opportunity of participating in control. . . . A private enterprise limits the possibility of personal participation by the eliminating device of the competitive process, but in a co-operative system there would be full equality of individual opportunity to contribute."

To Mr. Leonard equality of opportunity in its democratic form includes the right to become fit, physically, mentally and spiritually, to contribute to the common weal according to one's ability and aptitude—this through the fullest possible development of the individual personality.

Not conformity to some rigid pattern but adaptation to purposeful social change is an essential principle of this social philosophy. The song by J. A. Symonds with which the Co-operative Congress traditionally opens strikes this note of aspiration:

> These things shall be! A loftier race
> Than e'er the world hath known shall rise . . .

Internationally the co-operative movement sees danger in conceptions of national egotism and commercial rivalry. It supports the United Nations, free trade and world control of cartels. The rainbow flag that is displayed on International Co-operative Day represents in its seven horizontal stripes diversity in unity. The tendency of sovereign states in their modern form to devour all individuality of thought and action is rejected in behalf of a genuinely free world. The state itself is viewed as merely a relationship among men, subject to modification to conform to changes in popular needs and thinking. If the germ of a new social order is to be found in the co-operative spirit, the process will be one of decentralization, in which there is less representation and more self-government.

The desire remains, though dormant, for a thorough transformation of society, said W. P. Watkins, director of the International Co-operative Alliance. "To speak of the Middle Way is an understatement," he believes. "Co-operation is a third dimension, giving substance to democratic rights. It is not simply a means of avoiding state socialism or communism in the revulsion from individualistic excesses or monopoly. The positive element is mutual aid, by which certain principles are brought into fuller expression to meet the needs of a world shaped by modern technology."

# [ VI ]

# HUMAN RELATIONS LABORATORY

## 1. Roots in the Past

WHAT Beatrice Webb has called "the fascinating conception of the self-governing workshop" dominated the early years of the co-operative movement. The original goal of the Rochdale Pioneers was the establishment of a self-sufficient community on co-operative principles. This objective was set forth in these words:

"That as soon as practicable this society shall proceed to arrange the powers of production, distribution, education, and government, or in other words to establish a self-supporting home colony of united interests, or assist other societies in establishing such colonies."

Workingmen in those days could not forget that not long ago they had owned the tools of their trade. Dispossessed by the industrial revolution, they groped in the back of their minds for some way to recover control of the machinery of production.

William Morris, John Ruskin and the Christian Socialists represented in varying degrees the producers' claim on society, and the consumer point of view developed with difficulty. Beatrice and Sidney Webb tell in their book, *The Consumers' Co-operative Movement*, of the gradual evolving of the Rochdale theory into consumer control of productive processes as part of the distributive function.

Even so, co-partnership still has firm advocates, and there are today some fifty productive co-operatives where the workers participate in ownership. Most of these are light industries, and some of the more recent have been set up by trade unionists locked out or on strike against objectionable conditions. The worker committees of management appear in general to be well satisfied to hold their own without any great expansion. When new capital is needed it frequently is obtained by loans or sales of shares to the retail co-ops.

Trade union membership is a requisite in co-partnerships, and in almost all cases pay, even without the bonus, is slightly above the union minimum. Distribution of the surplus in one of these, a printing concern, made after payment of interest on shares, brought a 10 per cent wage bonus to workers and a 5 per cent rebate to customers at the end of a year.

The center of this historic survival is Leicester, where the Co-operative Productive Federation has its headquarters. This group includes eight clothing factories and a large number of footwear plants as well as several important printing establishments. Other lines are architecture, building, film and publicity service and stevedoring. Production on a heavier scale is undertaken by the Leicester Carriage Builders and Wheelwrights and the Walsall Locks and Cart Gear Society. A review of statistics by the Co-operative Union indicates that forty-five companies with 6,062 workers and share capital of $2,290,000 had trade exceeding $18,-000,000 in 1952. Wages were more than $5,000,000, and the surplus $691,000. Loan capital is listed at $2,613,000, reserves and insurance funds $3,691,000.

At the invitation of Arthur E. Jupp, secretary of the Productive Federation, I had joined a trade deputation from London Co-operative Society on a plant tour. The first stop was in the men's division of the Kettering Clothing Manufacturing Society. With six members of the management committee of LCS in tow, the manager's discussion was practical rather than theoretical. The Londoners appeared more than willing to expand dealings with the tailoring works, which does not, however, have the capacity to supply a trade of that size in full. Nor is the labour supply available in spite of outstanding welfare provisions including medical attention and, for women workers, marriage grants of from five to ten pounds.

The spirit of thorough craftsmanship is slow to yield to the pressures of mass production methods. As things stand today, the Kettering manager explained, every employee after serving an apprenticeship of several months has mastered the needle trade. But in rival establishments operated as profit enterprise, craftmanship had been abandoned, each operation being limited to three minutes. This elimination of a long period of low-paid apprenticeship has attracted the already short work force to these competitors.

The two women directors in the LCS party were interested in the coats and dresses manufactured in a separate building across a narrow road. They lent an ear also to the spokesman for Queen Eleanor, a co-op that seems to have turned from corset making to what is termed "lovely lingerie." This was at a luncheon with executives of several other co-op factories. In a little speech at the end of the meal he admitted that a workers' productive society had little chance of survival unless backed by the capital, credit and orders of retail co-ops. The co-partnerships, unlike the consumer stores, could not admit members beyond the capacity of the market to absorb their production.

The investment account of LCS shows approximately $3,000 in shares of Queen Eleanor, and shares and loans in Kettering Clothing to about the same amount. The balance sheet of almost every large retail society shows similar accounts, both Derby and Portsea Mutual, for example, having about $1,500 in Kettering Clothing works and smaller amounts in various shoe factories, Wigston Clothiers, Ideal Clothiers and the like.

As Mrs. Webb has noted, from time to time co-partnerships may fall into difficulties. Even when starting under full ownership by the workers, they are usually infiltrated by heirs and others having no desire to work there. About 40 per cent of the share capital is now held by outside individuals and by other organizations, mainly retail co-ops but including a few trade unions.

Labor union leadership, however, is wedded to the wage system and has no great love for co-partnership. It asks no share in the ownership of machines, even of those displacing manpower. A report on "workers' control" by the general council of the British Trade Union Congress dismisses any such idea as "out of date." There is accordingly no pressure for employee representation on boards of management, even in nationalized industries.

In an earlier day T. W. Mercer, writing on joint ownership, looked to "emancipation of all workers from servitude to any authority other than their own, and the abolition of the wage system, which is itself the evidence and proof that they are wearing chains."

The retail co-ops, as federated in the Co-operative Wholesale Society, own many productive plants under a different arrangement. To a certain extent the CWS factories and those in the Co-operative Productive Federation are regarded as competitors. Several worker-owned ventures involved in financial difficulties have been bought up by CWS, a process of absorption that has aroused some bitterness.

The profit-sharing sector would like to consider itself an experimental laboratory for industrial democracy. Suggestions have even been heard that the consumer-owned industries of CWS should develop works committees through which employees would participate in policy making. However, these and the further idea of transforming some CWS plants into co-partnerships have fallen on deaf ears. Beyond investments by retail co-ops which also constitute the co-partnerships' chief market, no progress has been made toward closer understanding. In fact, the secretary of one worker-owned concern has complained that its three largest shareholding societies have given no orders for three years.

There are, however, six plants in which co-operatives own considerable interest but are content to leave all policy making to those active in the business. One of these, the Kettering Boot and

Shoe Society, has a board made up of eight workers. Since the founding of the federation in 1882 there has never been a strike. The system in broad outline is one in which the workers hire capital instead of capital hiring the workers. Investors receive a fixed return, and any increased productivity on the part of the workers would be entered to their own credit.

Even an economist such as Prof. Cole sees some advantage in this over the prevailing method by which labour efficiency redounds mainly to the increase of the pofits of the proprietors, who have no share in the work. In a recent address to co-op educators in London, Prof. Cole placed great store on the future of co-partnership. In the right sized industries, he thought, it presented an alternative to nationalized boards, and to "the colossus that was the CWS."

Similar hopes are voiced by Mr. Jupp, who has his eye on industrial buildings erected by the state for lease to new enterprises. "I wonder how much thought the Labour party has given to a partnership between the state and the workers," he says. If in the future a government should decide to compete with monopolies, it is his suggestion that the job be leased out to groups of workers willing and able to function co-operatively.

It has remained for Emmanuel Shinwell, a member of the late Labour government, to carry this idea into political discussion. Co-operative partnership, he said in a speech, is more suitable than outright nationalization for industries such as clothing, boots and shoes, furniture, furnishings and certain chemical and electrical manufacture.

Meantime, Ian Mikardo, Member of Parliament for Reading and a chief lieutenant of Bevan's left-wing group, holds out for the industrial supremacy of the state. In an appearance which he evidently did not know was to be reported, he declared that except for interference by the Co-operative Insurance Society Britain would have a nationalized system of industrial insurance.

"The plain fact of the whole matter is that the co-operative movement is now a piece of commercial organization," he responded in a question-and-answer period. In its relationship to the community he found it difficult to distinguish between private enterprise and co-operatively owned undertakings.

These ominous words from a man prominent in the Labour party drew a quick response from the general secretary of the Co-operative Union, Robert Southern. Speaking at the Co-operative College he noted that not even co-ops could work on losses, and that nationalization of CIS would have absorbed a great deal of consumer capital while leaving other forms of insurance free to carry on non-industrial business.

"Co-operative societies are not operating in a vacuum and are not insulated against the effects of economic influences," Mr. Southern replied. "The aspect which distinguishes co-operative activity from that of capitalistic undertakings is that the ultimate net profit is distributed to consumers in proportion to their purchases."

The part which co-operative partnership is to play in production was questioned by the Webbs, who saw that the consumer federations had the advantage of producing for a known market. A realistic touch is added by Arthur Hemstock, himself an advocate of worker control, who writes:

It must not be assumed, however, that it is all plain sailing, for the acceptance of democratic responsibility is not a part of the training of the average man and woman, and as it would seem foolish to expect John Smith to step out of his office and fight Joe Louis without any previous training, so too, it is foolish to expect a worker, immediately he steps out of a capitalist factory into a democratically owned and controlled factory, to understand and accept the responsibilities involved, without any previous training and experience.

## 2. Increasing the Power to Consume

There is an element of the redistribution of wealth in the payment of patronage refunds. At least these repayments involve funds that otherwise might have been drained out of the community as profits for absentee owners. Particularly in the smaller and closer knit communities divi day is a gala occasion for everyone with anything to sell. Private merchants realize at such a time what a benefit for them is a little extra money in the hands of the working classes. Another fact to be noted is that the success of the British co-ops has not abolished these middlemen, but only limited them to their fair due.

A good deal of the payout is through branch stores but at Portsmouth there are some 13,000 members served through headquarters on Fratton Road. So great is the congestion at such times that the municipal corporation has to put on special busses. In one day almost $140,000 was either refunded or credited to members' accounts at this single point.

The patronage refund means new shoes for schoolchildren, coal for winter and, in recent years, "permanents" or some little extra comfort.

Service is the dominant motive of co-operation, and it is through the door of greater service that the cash trading principle of early Rochdale has disappeared. Gladstone in his days as Prime Minister praised co-operation as teaching "the working classes to pay ready money, and so tends to abolish the mischievous system of credit, and to encourage thrift."

There was even then a bit more to the theory, as George Jacob Holyoake wrote in *The History of Co-operation in England* back in 1879:

The definition of the co-operative principle in 1844 had assumed the following form: Co-operation is a scheme of shopkeeping for the working people, where no credit is given or received, where pure articles of just measure are sold at market prices, and the profits accumulated for the purchasers.

This able historian of the movement, whose tour of America in 1880 carried further information to large audiences as well as to such a distinguished few as Wendell Phillips, Emerson and Holmes, always stressed the point that credit was neither asked nor given.

With the acquirement of business experience the co-ops themselves no longer need to buy their stocks of goods for cash, having gained a credit rating of their own. This accession of confidence gradually has spread to the co-op membership. Under the extortionate methods of retailing in the hungry forties credit was a ruinous master, but today credit has been made the servant of a rising standard of living. That losses for nonpayment are small is a reflection of the pride and character of the co-operators. And always there is the nest egg invested in co-op shares to guarantee any debt.

There are in Britain, as in America, many families who do not have adequate equipment for efficient living. If one-third of American families still do not own an automobile, the proportion may well be greater in the United Kingdom. In the United States 45 per cent of the homes have no vacuum cleaner, 29 per cent no washing machine, 17 per cent no electric iron. Given adequate wages and such credit as is warranted, the potential market in any industrial nation for such household equipment as electric dishwashers, waste disposers, air conditioning units and electric freezers could provide peak employment in many industries.

There is as yet no visible limit to the power of production. Obviously, however, there are obstacles to increased consumption. Readily apparent is the basic need of an opportunity to earn. But something in addition to buying power is necessary to increase production—the desire to enjoy a higher scale of living. To an extent difficult to appreciate in America this collides with the ingrained acceptance of one's place in society, making a virtue of modest wants.

"In this climate we really don't need a 'frige,' " a departmental manager of CWS confided. An equally well-satisfied wife of a civil servant remarked, "I suppose by American standards you would consider my kitchen inadequate." And the woman proprietor of a first-rate private hotel: "We'll never have central heating—it's too dry."

As a nation Britain produces for export rather than for home use, except in the case of foodstuffs. Under such policy many articles of British manufacture are sold for less in other countries than at home, this partly in order to obtain dollar credits. Can it be that the contrary strategy of encouraging the home market would bring about higher production on a mass basis, and at lower costs, without diminishing to any degree the amount of surplus goods for overseas trade? Paradoxically, it is not more drudgery but more leisure that tends to stimulate the productive processes. Reduction in the hours of labor may encourage two beneficial results—leisure hours widen opportunity for consumer activities, and greater demand for goods and services is likely to increase employment and improve wages. An increase in wages, encouraging consumption, may result in larger profits.

The beginnings of this chain reaction may be discerned in the growth of co-op installment credit. Under pressure from Guildswomen a straightforward, economical method has been devised for acquiring radio and television sets, other electrical equipment and household furnishings. Latest statistics by the Co-operative Union list accounts owing by members of local co-operatives at $45,000,000.

Household convenience first postponed payment for deliveries of milk and bread from daily to weekly intervals. The middle-class system of monthly or quarterly payments has not been adopted. But housewives have gone far in modifying the ready-money principle. Back in the early twenties when co-op trade was languishing, many unfortunate families had to go to outside sources for credit, on most unfavorable terms. Complaints by the Women's Guilds in London resulted in the hiring of a number of women to call on members and offer them a new service to bring them back to the co-ops from private profit stores.

In a period of slack trade S. Foster, general manager of the London Co-operative Society, had knocked on a hundred doors in the East End to inquire about buying habits. How do you buy the family clothing? he asked. And what about household goods? Replies indicated that while food was bought for cash at the co-op, clothing was purchased through a private credit club. They were paying high prices for low-grade articles for which a door-to-door agent collected a shilling a week.

W. Henry Brown, who told the story in his book, *A Century*

*of London Co-operation,* recorded Mr. Foster's conclusion that mothers of families could not accumulate enough to make outright purchases. Some even confided to him that if they ever amassed twenty or thirty shillings in the house their husbands would fall into temptation to squander it on dubious pleasures.

Reporting "an avalanche of new trade" through the relaxing of cash requirements, Mr. Brown counted blessings also for those who paid cash, through more rapid turnover, newer and fresher goods and a reduction of overhead averages.

Two methods of organized and systematic credit are generally used. Hire purchase spreads installments on large bills over twelve months at 5 per cent interest. Payments qualify for dividend, which may offset the interest charge at year's end. A fire and life insurance policy is included without further expense. Of all co-op credit, $37,000,000 is for hire purchase and the second method, mutuality club debt.

The mutuality clubs constitute a system of weekly collections that now has lost any clubby semblance. Sixty per cent of the co-op trade in shoes and dry goods nowadays is through mutuality collections.

London Society's 366 mutuality agents are the missionaries of a consumer age, passing the collection plate. When a mutuality patron makes his second payment a voucher is issued for goods in the stipulated amount. One shilling, or 14 cents additional, is charged on each £1, this 5 per cent going into the collector's pocket. The further expense, estimated at 4 pence, is borne by the co-op.

Clothing, footwear, bedding and even coal thus are made available as needed. The system at the same time greatly expands trade in departments other than food. In September of 1953 this business at LCS exceeded $10,000,000. Bad debt losses over a ten-year period amount only to 2 shillings per £100, or .01 per cent.

Cash trading, as the young woman in charge of LCS mutuality headquarters observed, does not mean taking the goods in one hand and paying over the money with the other. At the same time she saw no advantage in encouraging indebtedness that members would not be able to support. Business sense did not admit of adding trade if it did not benefit the membership.

Average earnings of collectors amount to $1,500 a year, those oldest in service still being on commission, the others on straight salary. Some tour their districts afoot, others on bicycle, by motorbike or in automobile. One agent, now limiting his efforts, is eighty-one years old; among others are those with some disability requiring outdoor work. All of them, a grizzled veteran told me, function as propagandists for co-operation, and frequently fall heir to personal problems along their route.

"I kept on my rounds even during the blitz," he said. "The co-ops were more needed then than ever, and people who could not lay their hands on much ready cash still could buy what they needed, even if they had been bombed out."

His first approach to a new prospect is to tell some of the advantages of trading at the co-op. He mentions the convalescent homes, the loan of sickroom equipment and the divi. As he is on commission, he simply walks his beat in Paddington until tired, then knocks off for the day or retires to a little office where his customers may call.

"Except for unemployment or illness I have little trouble with my accounts," he continued. "A good many mothers have jobs outside their homes, and have to leave their children alone or with neighbors. Some do not like to trust a shilling with the young ones, and they hide the coins in odd places for me. At one house I am expected to go down a flight of basement steps to a beam over the coal hole. Others will place the money under a doormat, behind a certain flower box, or even hide it in bushes. At one stop the door key is hidden for me to walk in and pick up a shilling off the kitchen table."

### 3. The Search for New Incentives

The same persons are often to be found attending Labour party conferences and trade union and co-operative meetings. All three as social factors aim at enlarging the buying power of wages to keep consumption abreast of expanding production.

No economic system can function without labor power—or without consumers' spending power. Other ingredients of an operating society, including capital and management, can be hired or supplied privately or collectively. As a social philosophy co-operation is an end in itself, the framework of a new civilization in which the satisfaction of needs replaces the pursuit of profit. Nothing other-worldly is to be found in self-interest thus divested of exploitation, benefiting the many and doing harm to none.

There is a personality split, however, among co-operators themselves. To Conservative members the co-ops are a safety valve to prevent the explosion of the capitalistic system from the excesses of uncontrolled greed. This opinion also is common among Communists. At the other extreme are the Socialists, bent ultimately on state action and regarding co-operation as bearing the seeds of destruction of the old order.

The basic trade union makeup of the co-ops is reflected in benefits for employees which have set a higher standard throughout the distributive trades. In some cases wage demands are pressed on the co-ops which could not have been successful otherwise in outside employment. Yet clerks in the stores, asked if working in a co-op was any different from working elsewhere, generally indicated that such an idea had never occurred to them. Negotiators for a wage rise in the co-op laundries were frank in saying that to them here was just another commercial enterprise.

A problem not yet solved is how to turn co-op employees into ambassadors of co-operation. It has not been enough that CWS repeatedly has contributed to strike funds or that the stores have pioneered minimum wage scales and the weekly half holiday and even made union membership a condition of employment. Critics of the stores complain at times of a certain mateyness, referring perhaps to the absence of servility in the clerks. That the real difficulty lies elsewhere is indicated by a secretary-manager lecturing to a weekend class at Stanford Hall.

Impressing on management committeemen the need for a right attitude among the staff, he spoke of "bored and frustrated workers conveying their condition of mind to customers." The search must be for means to dispel, as he said, "that sour regard that hangs like a pall over all the opportunities we have for generating good will."

"We must really attempt to get rid of the role of the unloved employer and get our sales staff pulling with us on the same end of the rope at the same time," he continued. Among his suggestions were fuller discussions with the staff, letting the workers know the details of current distribution problems and sales policies. At the same time, he felt, more information should be given on primary co-operative theory and business economics.

The majority of workers, if they think about co-operation at all, he said, "regard us in our business organization as something of a band of well-meaning amateurs." But certainly, it may be put in here, these committeemen, serving year after year, some with on-the-job experience in the stores, are not lacking either in background or sympathetic understanding.

An outsider might venture the opinion that not enough executives are brought in who have had university or advanced technical training. Most managers, general and departmental, started with the co-ops on leaving school at the age of thirteen. This has its good and its bad points, one adverse factor being that most men are likely to resent orders from those whom they consider of no greater ability than themselves.

Reluctance to allow employees to serve on co-op boards has damaged morale. By now, however, more than one hundred societies have opened management committee posts to workers, though in several instances a limit of two seats is stipulated.

In defense of the consumer point of view, the charge is made that labor seeks domination, and not merely participation in management. One of those bringing this accusation was Frank Jones, long-time labor adviser to the Co-operative Union, recently retired. Calling attention to sparse attendance at some membership meetings, Mr. Jones noted that the organized employees may sometimes constitute a majority, and thus determine board makeup and policy. This to him defeats the consumer interest.

While shops in which no trade union contract has been signed remain open on Saturday afternoon, many co-ops do not. Galled by the consequent loss of business, Mr. Jones spoke slightingly of the overpowering desire of co-op employees to attend weekend sporting events.

Currently he had on his hands a walkout of milk roundsmen that left co-op members no source of supply but private trade. This dispute may indicate a lack of psychological skill in labor relations. The co-op had decided upon a change from truck delivery to what is called a pedestrian control vehicle. Drivers were not pleased with the prospect of dismounting and walking alongside the small electrically propelled cart. One of their number refused to give up his truck and was sacked, whereupon his associates, loyal to him rather than to the co-op, ceased deliveries until the official negotiating machinery was set in motion.

More than forty years ago CWS rushed a shipload of food to Dublin, thwarting efforts to starve out striking dockers, a dramatic demonstration of the solidarity of working class interests. Similar commissary aid was forthcoming in England's railway strike of 1920, yet misunderstandings continue to arise.

Most of the co-op employees outside production and transport belong to the Union of Shop, Distributive and Allied Workers. Its national president, Walter Padley, is a Member of Parliament and a frequent speaker before co-operative societies. The union's public relations officer, Cecil Hamnett, is a board member of Manchester and Salford Equitable Co-operative Society, chairman of the Co-operative Press and has a seat on the Central Executive of the Co-operative Union. Politically he is chairman of the local Labour party and a prospective candidate for Parliament.

What did Mr. Hamnett think about employee representation on management committees? To him the issue is broader, involving full membership rights for consumers who happen to work for co-operatives. USDAW takes the position that an employee who is a shareholder should be able to take his chances in a membership meeting on a basis of equality. Nottingham co-op, where the workers have an actual majority on the board, is flourishing. With the livelihood of the whole staff at stake what else could be expected? Bristol Society, with a $3,000,000 expansion program, has elected its first employee president—an inspector in the greengrocery department with forty years' service.

Mr. Hamnett did not believe that employees who are also members of a society should have board representation automatically. Some co-ops reserve a certain number of places on management for workers to fill. In such cases, he insisted, an employee elected directly by his fellow workers merely represents them, though a wider sense of responsibility should be involved.

Another question concerned the support given by agents of the Co-operative Insurance Society to nationalization of industrial insurance concerns, including their employer. Apparently this does not so much reflect dissatisfaction with CIS as with two other firms, Prudential and Pearl, whose collectors have never been unionized. Speaking now as a co-operator, Mr. Hamnett said these immense reservoirs of loan funds were financing chain store competition. Mutualization, proposed as a rather hazy substitute for nationalization, Mr. Hamnett concluded, left too many loopholes.

Somehow the interview gravitated toward a comparison of the voluntary approach of co-operation and compulsory social devices. He expressed impatience over the apparent unwillingness of co-ops to take advantage of their opportunities in new housing developments. Under slum clearance procedure, local councils limited shopping sites, and it was in the power of Labour party majorities to give the co-ops a monopoly. In some areas he found individual grocers or even a multiple firm had succeeded in barring competition. Still the co-ops cling to the principle of consumer choice, that there should be two or three groceries, a co-op and a chain store or a small merchant.

The further reasoning of USDAW is made plain in its report,

*A Planned Distributive Economy,* which includes the following rather startling admission:

"Too large a part of the nation's manpower is engaged in distribution. Today the nation needs the maximum number of workers on production. If there were more workers making things and fewer workers were needed to distribute them efficiently, the standard of living of the people could be higher."

For a trade union consisting largely of shop assistants this is piling on surprises:

"Experience has shown that unregulated and unrestricted competition does not lead to maximum efficiency and economy in distribution, but to an unnecessary multiplication of retail outlets and middlemen and, in consequence, of overhead costs which impede attempts to effect economies directed toward reducing prices."

Distribution absorbs too large a part of the work force because there are too many retail shops and too many middlemen is the conclusion. Only when the fact is recalled that the smallest and least efficient distributors engage no unionized clerks does this position reveal itself as one of enlightened selfishness.

Coming to the discussion of a state monopoly of distribution, USDAW defends freedom of choice except in the case of standard commodities. The co-ops, in this view, would continue to compete with other forms as one version of socialized distribution.

Thus, processing and distribution of milk is pointed out for public operation as a standardized product. Three possible solutions include elimination of the co-ops from this field in which they now figure so largely; setting up a national milk authority to compete with the co-ops or having a national authority collect and bottle all milk for distribution by municipal agencies competing with co-ops. A similar competitive basis is suggested for coal deliveries. Slaughtering and wholesaling of meat also would be marked for public ownership and operation.

Mr. Hamnett has been instrumental in setting up a course in co-operative theory and practice for USDAW study groups.

Theirs indeed is a challenging problem, and in free discussion no
mind can remain completely closed. At the same time new habits
of mind replace the earlier built-in certainties. If the real issue for
modern society is not collectivism versus individual or private
enterprise, a great deal remains to be determined—how much
collectivism is necessary or beneficial, and what shape it shall
take.

## 4. Of Course There Are Faults

British co-operators are not satisfied with the capitalist system.
They believe that consumer organization provides the most effective amendment. They are convinced also that many common
needs can be better served through state or municipal action than
under capitalism.

At the same time most co-operators oppose state operations
supplanting their own voluntary organizations.

While officially the movement is allied to the Labour party,
its membership embraces people of every political opinion. Some
burn with the crusading flame of old-time Socialists, others have
the attitude of modern Socialist intellectuals. In strong contrast,
but still sound in co-operation, is a Conservative element. An
underlying stratum is composed of men and women without any
political affiliations but with sufficient grasp of public issues to
weigh the pros and cons and vote according to their decisions.

Those who aspire to leadership in the movement frequently
possess clear-cut ideas on the relationship of co-operation to the
state and to the Labour party program. Yet neither these committeemen nor the rank and file are the ones responsible for the
detailed administration of co-op affairs. This is in the hands of
general and departmental managers, secretaries, accountants and
other professional men. These frequently do not hold strong
views on political affiliations, or if they do, remain inactive.

In the British civil service traditionally no one takes a prominent part in political campaigns but all support loyally whatever
government is in power. Like the civil servants, many co-operative officials remain aloof from partisan action. There are few

who combine an interested or enthusiastic approach to political and social problems with a flair for business administration. In the main these executives take the view that in the busy world of today they have quite enough to do in running their departments efficiently. This often leaves the Co-operative party political figures in isolation.

Why does the co-operative movement fail to exert an influence on public affairs commensurate with its size and economic importance? The *Co-operative News* in 1951 put that question to several men and women well known in public life. No consensus was found, although replies from Conservative politicians made much of the error of partisanship linking the movement with the Labour party.

Sir Herbert Williams, M.P., wrote: "The co-operative movement is of course a specialized form of capitalist enterprise, which a lot of people like to indulge in. Most unfortunately this capitalist enterprise has been captured by the Socialist party, and accordingly it attracts a great deal of hostility that would otherwise not be the case."

Another Conservative M.P., Sir William Darling, who started life as a co-op employee of St. Cuthbert's Society and now owns a splendid store in Princes Street, Edinburgh, also said that the association with one party has been disadvantageous to what he called "the co-operative trading system." Other business organizations, he maintained, "are at any rate less definitely political," and therefore stronger in their appeal.

Vyvyan Adams, formerly a Conservative member of the House of Commons, and the author of a pamphlet most favorable to the co-ops, expressed his hope for the future in this way: "The movement was conceived at Rochdale as something apart from politics. Today, through its alliance with the Socialists, it is threatening its own existence, because nationalization will mean the extinction of co-operation. The millions of Conservative and Liberal co-operators should stir themselves to free their societies of Socialist control."

Dr. Maude Royden, the famous preacher of London's City

Temple, compared the gospel of co-operation as preached by Toyohiko Kagawa of Japan and suggested that the British promoters, "after the first glow of pioneering had died out, have been too much occupied with its commercial success, and that there is in consequence a lack of the force of idealism which still, to a large extent, animates both trade unionism and the political Labour party."

Lord Amwell, a Labour Peer, stressed the significance of voluntary consumer co-operation as contrasted with a producer economy, and added a bit of advice: "You don't choose or pay your buyers properly. You are too proletarian and pay-packet minded. There are some things I cannot buy at the co-op, and I am not so choosy as all that, if I am a lordly person."

Kathleen Lonsdale, professor of chemistry in University College, London, a member for twenty-two years, "would regret any extension of the work along political lines."

On the other hand, Lord Boyd Orr, former chief of the Food and Agricultural Organization of the United Nations, has this to say: "Though I think the co-operative movement has been a highly successful and most important social movement, and also think it has not played the part it might have done in politics, I am not sufficiently well informed to offer suggestions on how it should move to exercise more influence in public affairs."

Reginald Arthur Smith, editor of the *British Weekly*, has "never been entirely convinced of the genuineness of the idealism expressed in consumer co-operation," which he regards as essentially a device for saving money for oneself.

So it appears possible to live in Britain and know little or nothing of the co-operative movement and its significance. One may even be a member and know scarcely more than where to find the neighborhood shop. Attendance at a general meeting, except on the occasion of internal differences, is usually small, though this is the fountainhead of authority. How many are capable of understanding a balance sheet as it is presented semi-annually may be even smaller.

Actually, in almost every society, as in a church or a labor union, there is a hard core of members sufficiently interested and informed to discuss the report of the management committee and able to choose capable men and women for committee posts. A considered estimate by Director W. P. Watkins of the International Co-operative Alliance counts an active 2 per cent who attend meetings. Dividing membership into three classes, Mr. Watkins, who for many years was a lecturer at the Co-operative College, lists those who stand for election and share in policy discussions in the basic 2 per cent. He speaks of an interested 3 per cent who follow their society's affairs in the press and other ways. A final category of the indifferent or apathetic 95 per cent is said to "take all the benefits but make none other than a cash contribution."

In such a situation initiative quite easily might pass to the co-op employees until what had been a consumers' society would find itself governed by a board whose primary interest was that of wages. Mr. Watkins cites one co-op in the north where employees packed a general meeting to vote themselves a bonus on wages equal to the member dividend on purchases. Without judging the justice of such an arrangement, still it is clearly possible that a large, cohesive staff can effectively obstruct policies designed for the benefit of the general membership. A departmental manager who has a subordinate on the board of management sometimes has a difficult time, and even now some committeemen have lost their seats as not sufficiently pliable to employee pressure.

A tendency toward amalgamation of small societies for the sake of efficient merchandising is further weakening democracy and eating away local community control. Small units continue to exist because of their age and reserves but are incapable of a wide range of services. Their trading areas may overlap and some of their historic sites are left behind by shifts of population.

In the Manchester area itself there are still seven separate societies, all with deep historical roots, largely in the old residential quarters, and with no central location in the main shopping center. Here, as in many other places, hidden assets have been accumulated through the years by consistent depreciation of the book value of fixed assets. A great deal of property carried at only nominal figures is still serviceable. Preliminary discussion of consolidation at Manchester reveals an aggregate membership of 300,000 and trade exceeding $47,000,000 a year.

Only 11 consumer groups have more than 100,000 members. At latest report, 41 co-ops, each with over 50,000 shareholders, constitute 45 per cent of the total national membership of 11,234,-718. There are 78 groups with from 20,000 to 50,000 members, comprising the next 21 per cent. Another 222 societies with a membership of 1,000 or less add to a total of only 113,081, a number approximating the size of such societies as Nottingham, Belfast or Bristol.

Tourists in the picturesque Lake district, which was made famous by Wordsworth, Coleridge and a whole school of poets, may note co-ops at Windermere, Ambleside and Keswick. The last, with 2,300 members, has more than doubled its refund by installing grocery self-service and a traveling shop. Windermere, 1,321 membership, also pays a dividend of 1 shilling 1 penny on £1. Its bread supply is from a private bakery, and the manager is quite willing to turn over his small coal trade as a municipal function.

Though limited service such as this can make sizable savings the process of concentration in England and Wales as well as in Scotland has brought centralized ownership by CWS and SCWS in a number of communities. An effort to develop large-scale national advertising has encouraged the idea of fixing maximum prices not to be exceeded by member co-ops. Some astounding variations of charges for identical products exist, reflecting the efficiency of different societies or the hunger on the part of some for a high dividend at the expense of competitive pricing. There has even been a suggestion that CWS should be made supreme over its constituent local societies.

A recent effort to lay down a policy of decentralization through an inquiry committee has been at least indecisive. A proposal in a minority report to separate banking from the trading sector, though continuing ownership and control by CWS, was voted down. The member societies also defeated a plan to establish five divisions, each with its own executive committee, to supplant the present highly centralized CWS direction of such disparate lines as food, textiles, footwear, furnishings and hardware. Some improvements designed to adjust the functioning of CWS to new circumstances arising out of its own development and changed circumstance in the world were accepted. One of these favored in the voting was better co-ordination with retail demand to facilitate mass production and bulk buying, particularly in the dry goods trade, a weak link in the co-op chain.

A major defect thus far unmended is the lack of any effort to immunize consumers against tricky merchandising claims. Despite all the Guilds and other attempts at further education there are no such guides to consumers as those of Sidney Margolius and Mary Sheridan, and no service comparable to the reports by Consumers Union on good buys and bad ones for Americans. In all the publications of the Co-operative Press there is little verging on domestic science, home economics or even family budgeting. Questioned as to the possibilities of forthright consumer education, leaders fall back on the excuse that British libel laws would penalize any comparison of brands or values.

"British housewives need the benefit of consumer advice," says a headline in the *Co-operative News*. It quotes an article in the *Review of International Co-operation* that cites the benefit of such publications as the American *Consumer Reports*, protective measures adopted by Swedish co-ops and the housekeeping committees of the Finnish movement with their testing demonstrations, public opinion research and dissemination of information on quality and standards.

The *Co-operative News*, like its twin, the *Scottish Co-operator*, concentrates largely on affairs of trade and politics. A federation of more than eight hundred organizations composing the Co-operative Press owns one newspaper of general circulation, *Reynolds News*. Although this is the only co-operative publication allowed on the stands of the newsdealers association, it falls short of filling any real need.

In his role as chairman of the board controlling *Reynolds News* Mr. Hamnett of USDAW has not been altogether happy. "A committee of grocers can't run a newspaper," one editor said as he resigned. Viscount Alexander on a later occasion raised a storm in the Co-operative Congress by accusing the paper of naïvely following the Communist line on some political issues. Low-cost insurance policies issued to subscribers for a time boomed circulation, which melted away by tens of thousands when paper-rationing regulations forced the abolition of such premium offers.

*Reynolds News*, a Sunday newspaper, comes under constant criticism for the paucity of its information on co-operation and its lack of the consumer point of view. Mr. Hamnett's defense is frank and direct. The biggest thing journalistically is the *News of the World*, a Sunday journal specializing in life in the raw, and having 8,000,000 circulation. Similarly Mr. Hamnett points to the sensational Sunday *Picture Post*, which was able to add 40,000 lookers, if not readers, with a series of front-page photos of Marilyn Monroe.

*Reynolds News* has found that a bathing beauty displayed just where the newsdealer folds the paper for sale brings many sorely wanted purchasers. It has been necessary, however, to issue an explanatory pamphlet, *Co-operators in Fleet Street*, to allay the disappointment of co-op members who had hoped for something more, or less. Beginning with the premise that Sunday is a day of relaxation, "when people like to put slippers on their minds as well as on their feet," the apology continues thus:

This public taste for a lighter Sunday paper has grown up over three-quarters of a century. *Reynolds News* did not create the taste and it cannot by itself hope to change a situation which is the result of a complex of social and economic factors. Public taste in this respect will only be changed by raising the general level of education, by the improvement of social conditions and by easing the tensions and fears that trouble peoples' minds today.

Each person familiar with this situation will have his own comment. The famous Swiss co-operator, Mr. Barbier, was moved to write an article for the *Scottish Co-operator* in which he said this:

Co-operative press, what is your destiny? Will you march in front, informing, educating, illuminating the questions and the consciences, fighting hard and without hate? Are you destined to awaken the sleeper, to give back to him open eyes, the taste of bread and water, rid him of apathy? Or will you remain—wise press without history—half speechless, half dead, half blind, which refuses really to cry, to hear, to see?

The first duty of the press is to help adults to understand the world and to encourage honest thinking. If the co-operative press is not carrying the minds of ordinary men and women beyond the propaganda danger zone it is failing in its responsibility.

One of the more obvious bits of propaganda, heard in America as well as in Britain, is to the effect that co-operatives should be taxed more heavily. This is nothing less than an effort to use the taxing power to level off competitive advantage in behalf of private profit business. Ordinary business charges its customers a certain price for goods or services. The difference between the charge and the actual cost of the operation is retained by the proprietor as his profit. A similar transaction by a co-operative returns the difference between the price charged and the cost thereof to the patron.

This margin at no time represents income to the co-operative, since it is under contractual obligation to return everything above cost to its members in proportion to their patronage. The distinction between a savings dollar and a profit dollar has long been recognized by the United States Treasury Department. According to a finding by the Board of Tax Appeals, the position is thus:

Had the taxpayer given a customer (whether stockholder or outsider) a discount promptly after filling the order, no one will call it a dividend. If a rebate were given promptly upon the customer's business reaching a certain volume, the same conclusion as to its character would follow. To make cost estimates and adjust them at or near the end of each year returning the excess payment to the customer would not change the reasoning which leads to this conclusion. Nor should the fact that the customer is a stockholder materially affect the result.

Some businessmen fighting co-ops continue to maintain that evasion of taxation is the secret of their success, which threatens the existence of "taxpaying business." Consumer co-operatives are on safe ground in replying that they pay all taxes required of them and that savings to their members are justifiably free from business taxation because they are not income for the co-op, which is only an agent.

Beatrice Potter, later Mrs. Sidney Webb, reached a similar conclusion in her book, *The Co-operative Movement in Great Britain*, written back in 1893. Likening a co-operative to the functioning of a self-sufficient family household which in producing for its own needs neither buys nor sells and so is without any tint of profit making, she wrote:

Is it possible for an association of consumers to realize profits? . . . Now, the substitution of a body of consumers *in association* acting through their representatives, for the householder supplying himself and his family, in no way alters the fundamental fact that these persons produce in order to consume and not in order to sell. For the member who buys an article at the counter of the Store, the manager who orders and pays for a line of Leicester boots from the Wholesale Society, is simply depositing in the hands of the officer of the Association a sum to cover the expenses of trading and manufacturing which have been or will be incurred in the production of these commodities. . . .

The profit-maker is essentially the person who obtains a market for the product of his own or other peoples' labor. But in an association of consumers the market is secured; since the members are forced either to consume what they have produced and pay the cost of it, or become insolvent and give up housekeeping on their own account.

# [ VII ]

# ECONOMIC SUFFRAGE

## 1. Mobilizing New Hopes

IN COLONIAL countries, co-operation is often the first step in building a modern community where the old tribal society is breaking down. There again the social benefits are inextricable from the economic. In such ways do people learn the working of democratic processes—to stand by decisions, to work in committees and to accustom themselves to electoral methods.

I remember hearing Maurice Colombain, then of the International Labor Office, tell of being sent to North Africa to introduce the natives to co-operative methods. Once there he found deep roots of mutual aid in the customs planted by past generations, which he had merely to fertilize and irrigate. This same historic backlog, he was certain, could be found even among the most primitive peoples.

The two of us were in a party making a tour of American co-operatives. The caravan had stopped at a farmer-owned gasoline co-op in Wilmington, Ohio, when M. Colombain pointed out a sign painted on the wall behind the pump:

IN THIS AGE OF POTENTIAL PLENTY WE MUST DEVOTE OURSELVES, NOT TO THE ART OF GETTING OURSELVES AHEAD OF OTHERS, BUT TO THE GREATER ART OF GETTING AHEAD **WITH** OTHERS THROUGH ECONOMIC CO-OPERATION.

Even in this Midwestern community it was natural, he said,

that thinking of this kind should persist where harvesting the results of a year's farming historically was a neighborhood affair.

The international flavor of co-operation is evidenced by the makeup of an ILO team invited by the independent state of Burma to guide and encourage the movement there. The English member, A. C. Marriott, formerly of CWS, has the task of converting the government-controlled Civilian Service Supplies into a wholesale co-op. Previously he was lent to the Anglo-Iranian Oil company in Persia, where he organized some 7,000 native workers into seven co-operatives.

A second team member is an Indian, K. Ayyer, assigned to organize industrial co-ops.

Cecil R. Crews, the third, was on leave from the Consumers Cooperative Association in the United States. His job was to train leaders to carry on consumer stores. With the help of a translator he has drawn up a book of lecture outlines for a seminar course and also written a textbook for Burmese schools. At latest reports there were 7,230 "concos," as consumer co-ops are called; 3027 "procos"; 177 "indussos" and more than 600 others.

A letter from Rangoon tells of nine young men leaving for advanced training in Ceylon and India—"to see and observe and, I hope, to return with a fire kindled within them—a fire that will not be extinguished for years to come."

"If these men catch hold of this great idea and enlist others, then I shall feel rewarded," the writer continued. "The urgency in Asia is here. The winds that blow across the minds of these people are often wild. . . . All Asia is a hotbed of revolutionary change—things boil here, they do not simmer. Our movement is needed, if for no other reason than to steady down minds that are stimulated too much, and to act as a school to train people in the arts and economics of business."

Lady Hilda Selwyn-Clarke of the Fabian Society Colonial bureau, in her pamphlet, *New Hope in Asia*, makes the point that the peasant craves security over the whole economic and social range. As a new way of life, co-operation offers an alternative both to Western capitalism and to communism.

"The first need," Lady Hilda says, "is to organize the credit co-operatives to provide short-term loans from seedtime to harvest or long-term loans to buy fertilizers, improved seed, livestock and agricultural equipment. The second security is the establishment of the marketing co-operative to overcome the exploitation of the trader and, where possible, arrange long-term agreements with the government. Next comes the consumer co-operative to eliminate exorbitant profits on trade goods."

If the inevitable process of industrialization is to be carried on as a community responsibility, the thought is, many mistakes of Western finance can be avoided. The constitution of the new republic of Indonesia states that the national economy shall be organized on a co-operative basis. There community storehouses for rice exercise a restraining influence on living costs. In contrast was the colonial method of profiteering merchants who ran up the prices of goods people must buy whenever their income from copra or rubber rose.

The vice-president of the republic has appealed to all civil servants to give every possible attention to co-op development. Of 1,752 recognized Indonesian co-operatives, Java has 1,420 in addition to 670 that are unregistered. While there is no element of compulsion, the state does provide the machinery, funds and training to make a beginning. Primary societies are linked in central federations on each island, with credit coming from the Central Bank.

This matter of governmental intervention has drawn opposition from both commercial interests and co-operative purists who distrust the state. In colonies where political disaffection is strong, governmental intervention in behalf of co-operatives tends to make them a political football to be kicked about even by the merchants who are exploiting the population. The most that can be done successfully is to help the people help themselves.

Marjorie Nicholson of the Fabian colonial bureau in the study handbook, *Co-operation in the Colonies*, asks why should colonial people have to undergo unnecessary hardships when British experience has shown a way out.

"Why allow competitive capitalism to develop when a little encouragement and assistance might open the path to co-operation?" she writes. "Since governments are in a position to help, and since Britain can influence these governments, should not Britain use her influence on behalf of the common people?"

At all events, there went out a dispatch from the Secretary of State for the Colonies in 1946 commending co-operative development to the various authorities scattered from Asia and Africa to the islands beyond and between. Model legislation and bylaws were prepared and a traveling adviser was appointed. He was J. B. Surridge, who already had done remarkable work of this sort in Cyprus and Nigeria. Assisting him has been an advisory committee drawn from the British consumer and agricultural societies. By 1951 the number of co-operatives in the colonies had grown from 1,885 to 5,527, with membership of half a million. Consumer trade reached £3,000,000 a year, with 565 retail co-ops where there had been only 45.

Special bureaus have been set up in more than twenty-five territories to guide this expansion. West Africa has its own school for training leaders. Scholarship awards take many overseas students to the Co-operative College near Loughborough, where the Co-operative Union is building more dormitories.

Mr. Surridge, surveying the situation from his advisory post, considered Ceylon developments as outstanding. There, as in Pakistan and India, British inspiration had set the movement going before independence, with co-operative bureaus manned entirely by native officials.

Ceylon, as an independent commonwealth, advanced funds for a Co-operative Federal Bank in 1949 following establishment of a Department of Co-operative Development. A wholesale agency to buy goods from abroad dating from 1943 has now passed from state control to an independent board. There are now 7,200 co-ops, of which 3,430 are consumer societies. The scope extends to dairies, hospitals, cottage industries, transport and journalism. One multi-purpose society started with 80 members in 1942, now numbers nearly 4,000 and has 23 branches. Besides growing food and warehousing it, operations include a textile works, bakery, rice mill, electric power and even a bookshop and a bus.

Reporting on a tour of Eastern colonies, Mr. Surridge found fishing co-ops in Aden protectorate, designed to break the grip of middlemen, to supply short-term credit and to market the catch at reasonable prices. In Malaya rice farmers are helping themselves through 500 rural credit societies, grown from seeds sown by a colonial bureau.

Co-operative credit is an important first step toward freeing Asiatic peasants from usurers. At Bangkok in 1951 a United Nations commission met with a group known as the Far East Working Party of Experts on the Mobilisation of Domestic Capital. The deliberations, which were not limited to Thailand but surveyed various countries, found that massing the resources of millions of people of small means offered a way to finance a variety of activities designed to raise the level of productivity and purchasing power and "thereby the standard of living." To quote directly from the ILO account:

The aim of the consumer co-operative movement is to insure for members through the mobilization of the capital of individual commerce a non-profit organization which will provide a cheap and efficient supply of goods as dictated solely by their interests as consumers. With the expansion of the movement consumer co-operatives have been able to secure for their members both the economies of large scale purchasing and distribution and, by entering the field of production, enable members to have supplies of manufactured goods practically at cost.

Stating that co-operation has a range of potential activity as wide as the business of life itself, ILO stresses the patronage refund as a further form of saving and speaks of the common interests building democracy.

This is not altogether new; in 1900 the British Co-operative Congress urged Joseph Chamberlain as Secretary of State to back enabling legislation for co-ops in the West Indies. He then called upon the Co-operative Union for information which he passed on to Jamaica and other outposts. Thus spread what in Cuba is described as a social and economic revolution that has never spilled a drop of blood.

Experience of United States authorities in Puerto Rico demonstrates that money alone cannot insure the success of co-operative efforts. There throughout the depression and during World War II every assistance was available for setting up both rural and consumer co-ops. These were regarded simply as business institutions with no reference to any social implications. What happened started a search for missing ingredients.

After two-thirds of the associations had failed, the University of Puerto Rico brought in an expert from the outstanding Nova Scotia development. A summer course taught by the Rev. Joseph Alexander MacDonald, who came from St. Francis Xavier University in eastern Canada, moved even the island legislature. A delegation of co-op leaders was sent on a tour of the Maritime provinces, and their report resulted in creation of a Department of Co-operatives as part of the extension work of the University of Puerto Rico.

The resulting legislation was designed to overcome two major deficiencies as defined by the inquiry. One of these was the lack of any properly defined social orientation, and the other the absence of any membership educational program in the philosophy and functioning of co-operatives or in the rights and duties of those belonging to the movement.

The new legal provisions called for an official inspector and further provided that Rochdale principles must be followed. A general meeting must be held each year, of at least 20 per cent of the membership. No member can serve on a board of directors for more than two consecutive terms, and each co-op must use at least 0.1 per cent of its annual business volume for education.

Consumer co-ops there now have some 8,000 members and annual trade in excess of $4,000,000. A credit union act has resulted in spectacular progress in protecting the people from loan sharks through the simple device of pooling their savings for lending purposes.

An attendance of 88 per cent of the membership at one annual meeting is reported by Luis A. Suarez in a paper read before the Rural Sociological Society of the United States.

"These associations," he sums up, "are important to their members not only for the economic service they render, but also as a kind of 'school of human relations.' Especially in the rural areas, the consumers' co-operatives are serving as instruments through which the people learn the importance of self- and mutual help."

## 2. AMERICAN VISTAS

The great days of American co-operation will come when farmers, now functioning through marketing co-ops, manufacturing and processing co-ops and purchasing co-ops, realize that they, too, are consumers.

In the end we may find ourselves better off than if the entire approach to consumer co-operation had come through industrial workers as in England and Europe generally. The progressive tradition of American farmers, a product of the pioneer spirit, has encouraged the use of the Rochdale formula, far in advance of the Tory tendencies of British agriculture.

Jerry Voorhis, executive director of the Co-operative League of the U.S.A., credits rural co-operatives for the electrification of nearly 90 per cent of the nation's farms. This, of course, was through a system of government loans and technical assistance in which farmers were helped to help themselves. Farm co-ops own 20 oil refineries and more than 2,000 oil wells. Mr. Voorhis estimates that co-ops distribute about 16 per cent of the petroleum products used on farms, and sets the figure for the Middle West at 22 per cent. Almost one-fourth of the fertilizer is produced and distributed in the same way.

A double-page display advertisement inserted in the *Editor and Publisher* by the Co-operative League states that 11,000,000 American families own stock in co-operative businesses, "three and one-half as many as own stock in all corporations listed in the nation's stock exchanges." Governmental reports show a gross annual business of about $10,500,000,000 for agricultural co-operatives. About three-fifths of all marketing co-ops now handle some farm requirements also. One-fourth of all crops are marketed co-operatively and similarly about the same proportion of farm supplies is so purchased. Feeds rank first in value, $897,-000,000 a year; petroleum products second, $574,000,000; fertilizer and seed following in order. There are almost 10,000 farm co-ops with an estimated membership exceeding 7,000,000, and about 160 mills, factories and processing plants of various kinds.

Politically co-operatives in Canada and the United States are neutral, depending on lobbying and pressure tactics for their defense against legislative attacks. This approach has done very well for the farm sector, but has accomplished little or nothing for the urban movement. The very process by which the government has encouraged rural societies has retarded expansion into urban communities.

In the co-operative marketing boom of the early 1920s farmers were convinced that they would be able to set their own prices through organizing gigantic commodity co-ops. Failure of this attempt finally resulted in more attention to reducing production costs through co-operative purchasing of supplies and equipment. Further economies were discovered in manufacture of such articles as milking machines, gasoline, oils, flour, feed, fertilizer, lumber and a multitude of other things. When farmers speak of themselves as producers, they are thinking of their crops. For a farmer to think of himself as a consumer has been hard enough, but he is even less apt to realize his remarkable record as a producer of non-agricultural commodities.

Funds salvaged from President Herbert Hoover's Farm Board sufficed to set up twelve regional Banks for Co-operatives as part of the relief measures taken by Franklin D. Roosevelt. These Banks for Co-operatives furnish credit for farm groups only. No federal funds are available for the strictly consumer services of the slower growing city co-ops. Genuine farm co-ops distributing such items as groceries to townspeople are not eligible for loans, on the ground that their purchases are not for farm use. A borrower may qualify with as much as 49 per cent of its business done with or for non-members, though these presumably are all farmers. Tax concessions granted to farm groups observing certain restrictions depend on a strict limitation worded thus in the statutes: "provided the value of the purchases made for persons who are neither members nor producers does not exceed 15 per centum of the value of all its purchases."

Dr. Warbasse, walking with a group of Ohio farmers to a meeting hall, asked who was expected to attend. This is the conversation that ensued:

FARMER. I should say about one-third producers and two-thirds consumers.

J.P.W. Who are the producers?

FARMER. The farmers, of course.

J.P.W. Who are the consumers?

FARMER. Mostly people who work in the factories here.

J.P.W. Aren't the farmers consumers; don't they consume about as much as these other people?

FARMER. Well, everybody knows the farmers are producers.

J.P.W. Don't these people in the factories produce anything?

FARMER. Yes, but they represent the town consumers.

J.P.W. Well, don't you think they are both pretty much in the same boat? The farmers consume the tires these town people produce, and the town people consume the food the farmers produce. Why can't they get together as consumers and work together to get the things they want?

FARMER. Well, I suppose they could, but the farmer is a producer and he wants good prices for what he raises.

By this time the party had reached the door of the hall and during the course of the evening it was Dr. Warbasse's task to try to clarify this ancient confusion. Nowhere in the world is there greater opportunity for close functioning of farm and city co-operatives to simplify distribution.

"The role of producer co-operation is well established in the United States and Canada, where consumer co-operation has not taken full root," observed General Secretary Southern of the Co-operative Union. "I think the reason is that traditional co-operative developments as in England have been from small beginnings. In this new era of standardization, intense competitive selling, and large-scale operation it is difficult even for convinced co-operators to begin trading operations on a sufficiently large scale to show the economic advantages which have been an outstanding feature of British co-operation throughout its history."

"Your farmers are getting there," he continued. "Major progress will begin when co-operation in its many forms and for its own sake is understood to strengthen the spirit of individual freedom.

"The first spate of political socialism in this country saw the emergence of public corporations to run a number of the basic industries. Under state monopoly conditions new problems have arisen. In part this is because economic democracy has not been accomplished in operating the nationalized industries, and partly also that workers in each nationalized industry have only one employer to deal with, on whom pressures can be brought with little concern for the public well-being.

"Furthermore, the consumers of the nationalized products and services get into a state of feeling helpless against the colossal organizations that have emerged. Consumer indifference is a bad thing. Real social strength must rest on individual responsibility and individual participation in all phases of life. State enterprise can emerge from political action but it breeds a state of passivity which is good neither for enterprise, efficiency nor real social strength."

Co-operative action as a form of social service strengthens character and accomplishes full responsible citizenship, Mr. Southern believes. He credits the British consumer movement with preserving the spirit of individual freedom through mutual association for collective action.

"Fascism and communism breed out of the indifference and inertia of the masses," he reminded us. "And everything which encourages creative effort and self-reliance must lessen the prospects for the development of those great evils which afflict the world."

The significance of the British experience is viewed in much the same way by Mr. Southern's opposite number, Executive Director Voorhis of the Co-operative League of the U.S.A. Next to hydrogen bombs, Mr. Voorhis says, the great underlying danger of our time is the loss of the ability and perhaps even the right to share in decisions not only affecting our fortunes but our very lives.

"I do not know of any device whereby the initiative can be restored to the people at the grass roots level except through the co-operative way," he adds. Ten years as a member of Congress did not leave Mr. Voorhis deficient in political knowledge, but in spite of, or because of, this experience he has never advocated anything but strict political neutrality for the American movement.

"Producer groups, including labor unions as well as industry, and particularly monopolistic industry, and including also associations of professional people, frequently tend to promote restrictions on the particular goods or services which they provide," he continues. "Such a scarcity is of benefit to the particular producer group in question, but only from a short-range view. On the other hand, it might become disastrous to society on the whole if carried far enough. It is, however, hard to push string, and a government trying to induce full production against the brakes put on by those in the position to control an industry will have a hard time.

"On the other hand, a strong business organization belonging to consumers, whether they are farmers or urban people, has a natural interest in abundant production and distribution. This is what it exists to provide from an economic point of view. To the extent that such co-operative organizations belonging to consumers carry on a substantial proportion of the business in any given line they are able by their competition to assert the general interest of the people and to induce a full production type of economy without the necessity of state intervention."

The experience of Britain indicates to him that in those fields where co-operation is strong nationalization is not likely to take place.

"This, I think ought to be an object lesson for those in the United States who want to promote private enterprise and are against socialization," he sums up.

One of the considerable values of any co-operative effort is its contribution to social stability through the opportunity for working men and women to learn something of the conduct of business and finance. Another benefit lies in steeling the nerves of a considerable section of the public against false cries of wolf and red, Socialist or Communist.

For example, there are about 5,000,000 heads of families in the United States belonging to co-operative credit unions. Savings thus deposited provide a ready source of loans in time of need, at a rate of 1 per cent a month or less on the unpaid balance. With assets mounting above a billion dollars, these credit unions now do about 12 per cent of the nation's small loan business. The co-operative structure is simple, each credit union being formed within groups already having strong ties, as in a church, labor union or working force, Some of the strongest units are among municipal employees and postal workers. Deposits usually are made on the member's initiative, although some groups operate through payroll deductions. Shares will pay from 4 to 6 per cent interest, and there are insurance and other benefits through a national association. The larger groups have paid accountants but the smaller pay no fees. The only connection of the state with this purely voluntary system is the checking by bank examiners. And yet a spokesman for an industrial banking group singled out these credit unions as an illustration of what he termed "the increased domination of the government in the field of finance." He went on to tell a convention:

"The credit union was conceived in socialistic sin, fathered by a paternalistic government and, strange to say, is still being foster-fathered by large corporations and local governmental units in direct competition with taxpaying private business."

If credit unions are socialistic, they certainly have received support in strange places, including in many instances even banking employees. The oldest one in North America was organized forty years ago in a Catholic parish in Quebec, with initial deposits of $26.10; since that time it has made loans in the millions for the stipulated "productive, provident and other beneficial uses."

To a loan shark, any lowering of the cost of credit appears subversive. Wherever co-operation has proved an effective competitor of profit enterprise, the economic battle having been lost, the next hope of co-operation's enemies is in political propaganda.

What is happening around the world is that co-operation in its many forms is taking on more and more importance as a peaceful system for the voluntary distribution of wealth. In some areas the only other choice for an exploited people might be revolution. This point has been made by the Rev. E. Stanley Jones, widely known as a missionary, the author of *Christ's Alternative to Communism*.

"I believe now, more than ever, the co-operative movement is the door to the future," Dr. Jones has said in an interview. "What impresses me deeply is that in the co-operatives the people themselves are effecting for themselves these social and economic changes. That puts the responsibility where it should be—namely, on the people. It develops personal initiative while effecting social change."

### 3. Live and Help Live

"Men and women are only valuable just in proportion as they are able and willing to work in harmony with others," reads the inscription on the back cover of the Enfield Highway Co-operative Society magazine. Among the lessons for Americans in British experience is this: remarkably the consumer movement, itself the product of continued agitation, has so steadied down as to become an outstanding constructive force.

"Originally the idea of the Labour party, and of the Co-operative party as well, was to capture the state and use it for class advantage," says Jack Bailey, an Enfield member who also is secretary for the Co-operative party. "Now it is realized that something more is due—the end of privilege, but not any class advantage."

As a corrective for the errors of the old order, British co-operative growth has been natural, an organic process which given the same environment could not have resulted otherwise. Even now, when the refund on patronage is trending down, membership and trade continue to expand. Let's go from the general to the specific.

Certainly the annual distribution of $140,000 in dividends on purchases and interest on shares of such a co-op as the 13,000-member Dover and District Society is not without impact on the channel area. An additional $70,000 surplus is left in the treasury as a further investment. With one-fourth of the retail trade in its community, this comparatively small society has an investment account of $500,000, and since the inauguration of collective life insurance, has paid off $101,000 in death claims.

Any real evaluation, however, must take into account the inner significance of such accomplishments as a demonstration of strength through united effort. What is the strongest appeal of Rochdale to the average member or the man on the street?

Endeavoring to answer this question, for the American Institute of Co-operation, John K. Friesen, then of the Manitoba Pool Elevators, said: "Deep down, it may not be the patronage dividend at all. We may not hear it expressed, but I wonder if our real strength does not lie in the fact that co-operation, like democracy, provides shared power and shared respect for its membership. It gives the somewhat confused person a chance to keep the economic issues from getting lost in a jungle of misrepresentations. As a TVA official once put it: 'The individual, in co-operating with his fellows, becomes a more important individual.' "

This feeling of consequence may be accompanied by lower prices as a buyer, higher prices as a seller, safer credit at lower cost, death benefits to protect a family, more returns on savings or just better satisfaction of some other need, including independence from domination of the mind or pocketbook by some quasi-monopoly.

A few years ago an American industrial group paid for an opinion poll on co-operatives as competitors. Some of the inquiries appear to have been heavily loaded, conveying impressions and implications about taxation and governmental loan policies unwarranted by the facts. However, to the question whether the public wants co-ops to grow, 56 per cent of those interviewed favored expansion. Should the government help? To that, 49 per cent said yes, 40 per cent no. Government loans to co-ops were favored by 54 per cent and opposed by 36 per cent. "If the government loans money, it should have a say in how a co-op is run"—60 per cent of those interviewed said no, and 34 per cent said yes to state controls.

Sixty-six per cent believed that co-ops sell for less; 8 per cent gave the advantage to "private business" and 17 per cent saw no difference. Percentages of present and former members on reasons for joining co-ops brought several surprises—to save money, 36; belief in co-op principles, 35; desire for fellowship, 16; helps national economy, 8; to get service not otherwise obtainable, 7. Twenty-six per cent said they joined to get refunds, and 22 per cent "to get better prices for crops."

An interesting and important query omitted from this research questionnaire is whether distribution costs too much. In this margin between what growers receive for their crops and what consumers are forced to pay is to be found the main opportunity for co-operation in America today. Only about forty-five cents of the consumer's food dollar goes to the farmer.

When farm marketing can be thought of as the process of distribution and not merely as selling, then the speculative hills and dales of the business charts can be modified by new and efficient routes from producer to consumer. Those mountainous upward and downward slopes of the financial index, with their avalanches and abysses, can be regarded as the evidence of human greed inevitably and periodically overreaching itself. As the farmer's share drops, the middleman's take, particularly the income from processing, goes up.

Not the short-term but the long-time interest calls for a complete understanding by which agricultural co-operatives make common cause with an urban co-operative system, meeting at a point midway for processing and manufacture. It is highly significant that from time to time special interests through their spokesmen in Congress seek to assure that marketing will not lose any of its predatory nature. Political attacks on co-operatives sometimes are insidious, as in the proposal to require that farm purchasing co-ops limit their transactions to the handling of farm production supplies.

The proposal in itself is an admission that consumer co-operation is spreading in rural areas. Particularly is this true in sections where diversified farming is on the increase, as contrasted with highly specialized corporation farming. Family farms, being on a smaller scale, are able to hold their own by co-operating as consumers as well as producers. Commercialized agriculture, operating on a much larger scale, is much concerned about profits from workers as well as from land, from Mexicans, Puerto Ricans, Indians and the dispossessed in general. Large-scale operators may buy farm equipment and supplies such as seed, feed and fertilizer through co-ops to reduce operating expenses. But they are willing to pay the full retail price for consumer goods, partly as an example to urban consumers. Experience has led them to the belief that high retail prices usually mean better return for farm products.

Farmers are the backbone of co-operation in the United States, though they still exercise their legal right to charge all the traffic will bear and are inclined to view themselves as businessmen with the same rights and objectives as the grocer, hardware merchant or manufacturer. They have proved the economic advantages of co-operation but have scarcely been aware of the spiritual connotations. It is regarded as a tool brought into use when people confront the fact that they can render better service for themselves than they are able to afford by reliance on the ordinary machinery of distribution or production.

That it is something more is made plain by Murray D. Lincoln, president of the Co-operative League of the United States of America. In an address on *Co-operation and the Moral Crisis* at St. Francis Xavier University, Nova Scotia, Mr. Lincoln quoted E. H. Carr, a famous British political economist, who wrote in his book, *Conditions of Peace:* "Our civilization is in danger of perishing for lack of something for which we have dispensed for two hundred years but with which we can dispense no longer: a deliberate and avowed moral purpose, involving the call for common sacrifice for the common good."

"Too long," commented Mr. Lincoln, "have men of good will been timid and hesitant. Too long have we been bullied, bluffed and confused by those who would destroy but who will not build. It is time now—it has long been time—for men of good will to embrace their responsibilities, to speak out, to dare to be different and to use their capacities for working together in behalf of peoples everywhere."

As the active head of CARE, which distributes food packages and other necessaries overseas, he has shown the possibilities of a people-to-people program. And as president of the Farm Bureau Insurance Companies of Columbus, Ohio, he has demonstrated how pooling small resources can create credit and build co-operatives.

In acknowledging the award of a Doctor of Laws degree by the Nova Scotian school, itself the center of inspiration for co-operative effort, Mr. Lincoln expressed the conviction that powers and talents and virtues in mankind hitherto undreamed of can be unleashed by co-operation "applied politically, economically and spiritually."

Many American co-operators make the pilgrimage to Antigonish and the remarkable extension headquarters there of St. Francis Xavier University. The Antigonish movement is remaking the lives of the fishermen, farmers, miners, lumbermen and steel workers of Canada's Maritime provinces. Study groups

under its auspices have grown into more than 400 credit unions
with assets exceeding $7,000,000 in small savings. Freeing them-
selves from notorious exploitation, the United Maritime Fishermen have financed their own lobster canneries and fish-processing
plants. Self-help has been applied to low-cost housing, and there
are more than 150 co-op stores.

When Mr. Lincoln was head of the Ohio Farm Bureau Co-
operatives the example of Nova Scotia's discussion groups was
brought to the rural areas of the United States. The thousand
advisory councils of the Ohio Farm Bureau are the outgrowth of
the Antigonish principle that no sudden or revolutionary change
can solve the social problem.

For many years Monsignor M. M. Coady as head of the extension service of the Antigonish Catholic school, realizing that
habits are changed only by changing opinions, sought to raise
the whole level of knowledge and human values in the Maritimes.
Feeling that co-operation is a necessary part of economic life in
a democratic society, laying the foundation for real democracy,
he was still ready to concede that it was not necessarily the total
answer. On a lecture tour of the United States he said: "Group
action or economic co-operation will condition people to the
point where they can manipulate the other social forces in a
realistic way. The other forces, of course, are political, educational and spiritual. Co-operation is, so to speak, the ticket to the
great economic show of the future."

Competition in the sense of economic combat could not bring
peace and good will, in his view. Like the Scottish co-operators
who set the example for the Nova Scotian movement, Dr. Coady
feels the necessity for a certain degree of socialization, by which
term he refers to public ownership. Profit business, he observed,
would not electrify rural communities with power or even supply telephones in rural communities that would not add to its
gains.

"If the whole electric business were socialized, then profit that
is now being made in the denser centers of population could be
stacked up against the losses in the electrification of the rural

communities," he said. It might be possible for a government to generate power to be distributed through co-operatives, he continued. Conceding that there might be other fields for public ownership, he disposed thus of across-the-board nationalization:

"It would seem bad logic, however, to advocate socialization because the people are not competent to run co-operatives efficiently. Running co-operatives would seem to be a simpler job than running a socialist state. By what magic can the people who are incompetent to make co-operatives work become so efficient that they are going to run the more difficult state? It is conceivable that long training in co-operative activity can make the people capable of running a socialist state, but in that supposition they would not need it. The problem already would have been solved.

"If the people are going to develop this great efficiency by the magic of suddenly turning socialist, it is to be feared that the instrument of the efficiency would be bureaucracy and coercion. It would seem to be more in harmony with the psychology of the Anglo-Saxon peoples to do it the co-operative way."

Man having learned how to co-operate with his environment, whether in Nova Scotia, the British Isles or Midwestern America, may yet learn to co-operate with man to overcome individual limitations. There can be no real freedom without organization, whether of the state or some comparable institution. The most interesting thing about Father Coady's leadership is the realization that the modern state must intervene with social controls. A major function of government, even of the Conservative pattern, is so to guide economic activities as to make anti-social practices unprofitable. And so anti-government prejudices can be carried too far, to the benefit of those who regard mankind as nothing but sales fodder.

If a proper function of the political arm is to help people to help themselves, then wider use of the principle of insurance by government agencies may be expected. Federal insurance of home mortgages, of bank deposits, of employment and social security have shown the constructive nature of this approach. Rapid de-

velopment of what electronics engineers call automation may
further enlarge production and decrease employment. If we are
to be saved from depression and the horrors of totalitarian dic-
tatorship it will be by widespread participation in the ownership
and earnings of capital, assuring a market to absorb production.

And so there is really no limit to the possibilities of co-operative action in the United states, and the wider its application the
better for all society. In the British co-ops no avenue of pooling
small savings is unexplored, even to a Christmas club collecting
3 pence a week, on which full dividend and an extra bonus of 1
shilling on £1 is paid. A thrift system under which stamps
bought at 3 pence each are accumulated on a card holding 40,
amounting to 10 shillings, allows opportunity either for trade or
transfer to the share account.

Such savings plans are too few in the United States, as Executive Director Voorhis of the Co-operative league pointed out:
"I think British experience might also be significant to America
for the manner in which people have been encouraged to invest
their savings, thus making available capital funds for the expansion of their own co-operative business."

"A co-operative is one of the few institutions people can use
to distribute abundance," the president of the Co-operative
League, Mr. Lincoln, said. "But because we are not Christian
enough or decent enough we have to go to war to distribute the
abundance. People have the tools in their own hands to control
and fashion their own destiny."

These remarks were made at a meeting attended by the managers of some thirty co-op supermarkets, many with a volume of
more than $1,000,000 a year. Host at this conference was the
Co-operative Enterprises of Akron, Ohio, representing a $500,000
investment, mainly by rubber workers and their unions. This
huge general store and a gasoline service station make sales of
$2,500,000 a year. There are many such current successes, from
Natick, Maynard and Fitchburg, Massachusetts to Palo Alto and
Berkeley, California.

Statistics are tricky when it comes to summing up the extent of American co-operative effort. Not only do many farmers belong to two or more co-ops, thus swelling membership totals, but also government figures overlap. Farm co-ops are checked by the Department of Agriculture, and urban consumer groups by the Bureau of Labor Statistics of the United States Department of Labor. A thousand or more organizations are entered in both categories.

How, for instance, is a general store combined with a farm warehouse to be classified? One typical unit operated by a rural association will have groceries, work clothing, electric appliances, feed, seed and fertilizer storage and perhaps a hammer mill, gasoline and oil station and even coal and lumber supply. The same agency may also market grain and ship out eggs and other produce.

No such doubts surround the all-purpose society operated by Bohemian miners around Dillonvale, Ohio; the thriving Hyde Park co-op on the fringe of the University of Chicago or the Greenbelt and other co-op services centered about Washington, D.C. These metropolitan consumer centers need closer relationships with their country cousins. Once mass buying power is possible, they need also an extensive system of manufacture on the British scale, but with more participation by agricultural co-operatives. Just as London co-operators bought up a chain of drugstores, so the American co-op leaders hope to purchase a grocery chain.

"It isn't true that there is no money in the grocery business," says Mr. Lincoln. "The best ones get their capital back twice a year."

The huge Akron co-op turns over its stock thirty-five times in a year, and is setting a fast pace for the chains. A fact little realized is that not these chains but independent local dealers originated the supermarkets which have revolutionized the food trade in the United States. The four-hundred-car parking lot of the Akron co-op is in high contrast to the chains of a few years ago, which relied on a multiplicity of small outlets for their profits. The founder of one chain which set up fourteen thousand branches once remarked that if each grocery returned one dollar a day above expenses he would have a good profit.

Still there is room for more efficient distribution from farm to table. Harold V. Knight, former editor of the North Dakota *Union Farmer*, recalls that at one time the Farmers Union proposed government loans for storage and processing facilities under a plan something like that of the Rural Electrification Administration for aiding power co-ops. These plants presumably were to be farmer-owned, but provision could have been made for joint producer-consumer distributive operations.

"The idea also was to make loans to labor-sponsored co-op stores to act as a safety valve to open or close the flow of goods from the storehouse to offset scarcity prices and profiteering," Mr. Knight says. "I think the idea would be sounder than government purchase of butter stocks, to cite one example. However, these loans were to be tied to an overall farm policy, and not just to promote co-operatives."

North Dakota from the days of the Nonpartisan League has been in the forefront of political, social and economic experimentation. A state-owned flour mill at Grand Forks has operated for years to assure farmers a premium for their hard wheat and in addition has turned back substantial earnings to the public treasury. Across the Canadian border in the neighboring province of Saskatchewan, the co-operative wheat pool has forestalled similar state intervention by erecting its own capacious milling and processing establishment. Neither of these plants fits exactly into the consumer pattern, though both serve as yardsticks by which to measure the costs and profits of what has threatened to become a private monopoly in the people's foodstuffs.

One of the early enterprises at Rochdale was a flour mill which long prospered under co-operative ownership. As formation of combines required larger operations the milling function was concentrated in the hands of the CWS as agent for all its members. This now has a yearly output valued at more than $37,-000,000.

Back of this tremendous production is the shopping habit of

11,000,000 Britishers representing, with their families, half the population. Nothing approaching this exists in America as yet. What keeps co-operatives from realizing their potential influence in the economy of the United States?

Six economists, endeavoring to answer this query, have come up with these observations:

People expect from co-operatives something better than they would get from other businesses.

Co-op leaders are too complacent, and among societies themselves there is unhealthy competition.

Local sections of the movement and the local leaders tend to isolationism.

Local societies do not buy all they can from co-operative sources, and regional associations have hardly explored joint operation.

The movement should develop new products and increase margins by ordinary commercial practices.

Greater education of the public is necessary.

### 4. A New World Made to Order

In the Trossachs a young Scottish woman manages the tea room of a co-operative store with the same spirit of dedication in which on Sundays she plays the organ for the village church services. In the industrial Midlands self-help associations have erected whole neighborhoods of houses for their own occupancy. Throughout the United Kingdom local distributive co-operatives have built homes for rental to their members, have made loans available on mortgages for home building or buying. At the same time local authorities have put up row after row of "council houses" designed primarily to moderate the burden of low income families.

Planned social progress is in a last ditch fight to prove that a more abundant life can be achieved without revolution. Collective control over social conditions, on a basis of justice rather than charity, takes many forms. Public ownership and management of all capital or of larger and larger sections of business have advocates who desire to end the ability of the strong to exploit the weak. A new set of human values is replacing the old ritual worship of power and success.

Political catcalls, endeavoring to cast discredit even on the process of thinking through the dilemma of modern society, are losing power. It is less possible to condemn ideas by mere name-calling or to defend outworn practices by slogans that somehow have lost their ring of conviction.

That pretty young co-op employee in the Trossachs reflects a wholesome climate of opinion and conduct which is socializing the individual and at the same time strengthening the spiritual outlook. To her co-operation means more than just a new economic system. In addition it involves and supports the brotherhood of mankind and individual freedom of choice as a way to shape history.

Consider also the "self-build" societies, of which there are now more than one hundred. The initiative here often comes from groups of war veterans who are determined to improve the living conditions of their families. After having obtained the agreement of their local authority, they begin training in building. When proficient, the members begin work under the guidance of a skilled foreman. Such groups endeavor to include some men already trained in plastering, plumbing, electrical installation and other building trades. Model units usually contain from thirty to forty men, each working approximately twenty-five hours a week on the site.

In helping these families to help themselves the local authority makes a mortgage loan of 100 per cent of the total cost, while members are required to hold loan stock, own a £1 share and make a weekly payment to cover running expenses. Under the provisions of the Housing Acts, a similar association can provide accommodation for able-bodied old people either by new building or conversion. Arrangement through the local authority with the national Exchequer brings a subsidy of £5 per bedroom payable annually for a maximum period of sixty years. In this case the local authority may lend up to 90 per cent of the cost of providing the hostel.

"Co-operation is Christianity in action," says Kagawa, its great Japanese advocate. "The economic foundation of world peace . . . the love principle applied to industry." Just as Christianity stripped the Caesars of their divinity so does co-operation, given proper consideration by the state, relieve modern government of many of the demands for collective organization of social and economic life.

"The state has always encouraged producers but asks consumers for sacrifices," Percy Redfern, the historian of British co-operation, observed. Now in his eighties, he had come out of retirement at Meadow End in Cheshire for a visit to Manchester, the co-operative capital and the base of his long career in pamphleteering. Cheering to him is the dawning understanding that the productive process should be carried on for the benefit of the consumer, a belief that lights up the horizon of man after the moonshine of reaction and the darkness of revolution.

"While the producer tends to exploit the consumer by restricting supplies, the interest of all mankind as consumers is in abundance," he resumed. "At no time need the consumer be helpless—even in the face of price maintenance agreements—and those retailers who have claimed some sort of divine right to levy toll on the distribution of goods now find the real test lies in service, quality and efficiency."

All consumer co-operative business, he pointed out, has for its end and purpose the satisfaction of human wants, "whereas every competitive business ultimately aims at profit and power." In a pamphlet, *The Consumer's Place in Society*, Mr. Redfern begins by saying that when a consumer buys without knowing who it is that sells, sometimes without knowing what the thing he buys under a fancy name really is, or where and by whom the article was made, or under what conditions, then he is helpless as a child. To quote directly:

And when a man works without even knowing who is the final owner of his place of work, and of himself when in that place of work, and without knowing or caring what the final value-in-use of his work may be to his fellow men and women, he is a serf. And this is intolerable, for either this breakup of human life will continue until the whole capitalist world follows the old slave empires to ruin, or human right and freedom will assert itself, and with revolutionary effect man will be set above money.

What Mr. Redfern is saying reflects indignation over the subordination of human personality which is typical of what is called private enterprise. The same vice of impersonality may also exist in a thoroughly socialized state. The co-operative spirit calls not for state confiscation but for the good use of wealth. To the extent that any privately operated business recognizes its obligations to the consumers and to the community as well as to its shareholders and workers, there is no quarrel.

If the paternalistic trend to the impersonal and bureaucratic control of the labor and life of men is to be halted then large industrial plants must function more nearly as self-governing local communities. Well-advised businessmen will not carry on a vendetta with the co-ops, which also represent private ownership. Indeed, the continued existence of private enterprise hinges on general acceptance of some such alternative to across-the-board nationalization.

The British spirit of fair play has been aroused against a car-telized economy. Objections to big business may lie less in its ability to make a profit than in its excessive power. In a parallel situation in the United States, the success of the American Medical Association in a political struggle against national health insurance has made the doctors' trust a prime target of slowly rising public apprehension. Only co-operative health care can provide a substitute in this day and age for what is called so-cialized medicine. Here as in Britain any extraordinary display of might by the giants of the profit system serves only to extinguish their last hope of escaping critical public attention.

A forthright position regarding a state-dominated economy is that of John Corina, president of the Co-operative Congress of 1953. Granting that nationalization was necessary in the basic coal, rail and power industries, which could not have met the nation's need without state capitalization, he still drew some limitations.

"But in the consumer field we say that the most workable system is the co-operative system," he said in his presidential address. "Our form of organization assures diversity of tastes, infinite variety and fluidity of conditions, together with integration and, above all, democratic control. *We cannot, therefore, agree to any weakening of this social fabric by the compulsory transference of consumer services to bureaucratic forms of state control.*"

"The modern state has quite enough to do without dabbling in the retail and wholesale business," Mr. Corina explained later as we sat in the board room of the Royal Arsenal Co-operative Society at Woolwich. "The days have gone by when you could fool the people with the idea that governments can do everything for the person. We must have new thinking on these problems. To do things for ourselves is to live. To leave the state to do it all is to resign from life itself."

Lopping off branches one by one would destroy the co-operative tree, he said in reference to suggestion that milk be declared a municipal utility and to similar plans for bread, flour and insurance. In Derby, Leicester and Nottingham the co-operatives distribute nearly 80 per cent of the milk supply.

Others of the Royal Arsenal Society board expressed their support of his stand. One director promised "the fiercest fight that ever happened" if the Woolwich authorities attempted to take over the dairy and bakery functions. This co-op, the second largest of the London area and of the country, has nearly 400,-000 members and refunds well over $2,000,000 a year to them.

RACS differs from ordinary practice by maintaining a full-time management board, elected by proportional representation. Five of the seven board members have been employees, resigning those jobs upon election. As a direct member of the Labour party, to which it contributes $39,000 a year, the society may be expected to carry more political weight than most other groups whose tie is with the Co-operative party alone.

"One pound spent at the co-op does more to promote public ownership than a thousand speeches in parliament or out," Mr. Corina maintains. "To the Labour party we say that none of their proposals for public ownership and control is as democratic as co-operative enterprise."

British socialism, which antedates Karl Marx, up to the present day has never concentrated its full hope on nationalization as an end in itself. There is a deeply religious undertone in its crusade for fair shares to all. The co-operative political movement in 1918 defined its incentive as "production for use and not for profit" and the economic basis of society as "the common ownership of the essential means of life."

The Labour party constitution likewise leaves the question of outright state ownership and operation open. The aim here outlined is "to secure for the producers by hand or by brain the full fruits of their own industry, and the most equitable distribution thereof that may be possible, upon the basis of the common ownership of the means of production and the best obtainable system of popular administration and control of each industry and service."

The emphasis on producers and lack of any direct reference to consumers lies at the source of current misunderstandings. It is plain, however, that even under this charter the socially owned sector may take a variety of forms, among them voluntary consumer and producer co-operatives as well as state ownership. For the matter of that, the rules of the Co-operative Union look to "the ultimate establishment of a Co-operative Commonwealth."

In his novel, *Endymion*, Benjamin Disraeli, Earl of Beaconsfield, introduces a character, Enoch Craggs, who was walking into Manchester for a workingman's institute, this in the Lancashire of the Chartist period. "I am not against capital," Enoch explains to the patrician but sympathetic Endymion. "What I am against is capitalists." This leads into the following passage:

"What can workmen do without capital?"

"Why, they make the capital," said Enoch; "and if they make the capital, is it not strange that they should not contrive some means to keep the capital? Why, Job was saying the other day that there was nothing like a principle to work upon. It would carry all before it. So say I. And I have a principle, too, though it is not Master Thornberry's. But it will carry all before it, though it may not be in my time. But I am not so sure of that."

"And what is it?" asked Endymion.

"Co-operation."

The capital letters are those of Disraeli. Now forgotten as a novelist, he did understand and portray the political and economic currents of his day. Out of this ferment in the working class the Rochdale Equitable Pioneers' Society developed. It is to be noted that the word "co-operatives" does not enter into this historic title—previous local ventures stranded on the shoals of credit and lacking the advantage of the patronage refund had cast a shadow on the term.

One unrealized ambition of the original Rochdale charter was the erection of a temperance hotel. Operation of co-operative restaurants has over the course of years led many societies to acquire liquor licenses and even to run public houses.

Discarded also is the final provision of the Rochdale rules already quoted: "That as soon as practicable this society shall proceed to arrange the powers of production, distribution, education, and government, or in other words to establish a self-supporting home colony of united interests, or assist other societies in establishing such colonies."

According to one bit of folklore, only the death at sea of one of the Rochdale founders prevented the establishment of a hoped-for colony in Texas. The American Civil War brought misery to the cotton weavers of Lancashire, but Rochdalers rejoiced at the freeing of the slaves. It brings these men and women of good will closer to recall their twenty-pound contribution to sufferers in the disastrous Chicago fire of 1871. Evidence of admiration for American ways is to be found even in the spelling of the co-op motto, "Labor and wait," without the English "u."

The Rochdale historical background is fading, even for fellow countrymen, as I found on a Christmas shopping trip in the south of England. Under a national arrangement a member of a co-op in another town can be credited for dividend purposes on purchases made in a co-op of which he is not a member.

In paying for my packages I gave the clerk my code number in the Rochdale Pioneers. "RP 23061," I told her. She wrote it down in triplicate but looked up inquiringly.

"It's Rochdale," I explained without evoking any sign of recognition.

"That must be somewhere up north," was her final response.

In spite of such lapses, there is a feeling of fierce loyalty to the Stores, an underlying spirit of self-reliance which lives in the present and not in the past. Occasional anecdotes light up this relationship in a humorous way. One concerns a small boy who had just heard that the doctor had brought him a new sister.

"There'll be a row when Dad hears it didn't come from the co-op," he predicted.

In another story a woman shopper inquires of a bus conductor: "Do you go to Selfridge's?" The conductor replies: "No, I prefer the London co-op."

A good-humored reference to the sometimes thankless task of sitting on a management committee tells of a dead co-op director who reported for entry at the pearly gates. St. Peter inquired his name, but returned later to say that there was no record. Protest resulted in a new search but without success.

"What did you say was your occupation?" St. Peter finally asked. "Co-op official," was the reply.

"Ah, that accounts for the mistake," said Peter. "I was looking in the Book of Saints; I should have looked in the Book of Martyrs."

I had seen Lord Williams, the president of the Co-operative Wholesale Society, in action some weeks before my farewell visit to London. The occasion had been a CWS membership meeting in Manchester attended by some 250 delegates from northwestern retail societies.

Now, public ownership may get too remote from the consumer of its services; not so co-operation as long as these membership meetings exist. At a long table behind Lord Williams, who presided, were seated various departmental managers whose role was to answer a flood of queries and face whatever criticism was forthcoming.

Making her way to the front microphone was a woman who explained that her family loved coffee, and why was it that every district except Manchester had received the new co-op instant brand? Following her was a delegate from Leicester with a complaint of excessive charges on direct billing of fish. Two men from Ten Acres and Stirchley Society led a losing battle to induce CWS to foot expenses of local athletic teams made up of employees in championship tests.

One may question at times whether democracy and efficiency go together, but when the dust of discussion cleared away, delegates from near and far had the answers they sought, had made their own points and in addition were able to take home to their management committees a new understanding of the importance of uniform pricing and national advertising.

"No, I don't think co-operation is dull at all," Lord Williams said in retrospect. "It's damned exciting."

Well, what about co-operation as a satisfactory form of social ownership? We were seated in the executive offices of the huge CWS headquarters in London, which alternates with Manchester for management meetings. I was quite prepared for his analysis, which followed pretty closely the non-political point of view.

"The out-and-out nationalizer believes in accomplishing his ends by the single stroke of legislation," his lordship began. "Co-operators have faith that in the long run their voluntary system of production and distribution will pay the better dividend in efficiency and in satisfaction for a job well done.

"We gave up our mining property without regret when the coal industry was nationalized, but there is no reason why we should not continue our retail function alongside any national or municipal home delivery system.

"If the government should take over the big flour milling combines, our integrated system in which co-op mills, bakeries and retail distribution are meshed should not be disturbed.

"And in the matter of milk, the question to be decided is which method is more efficient. If co-operative distribution were allowed to continue and to pay a dividend to consumers while a nationalized dairy business did not, there is no question which form would take precedence over the other."

Once only the privileged classes were ranked as consumers, and all the rest simply as producers. In the new age of potential abundance it is plain that the task of distribution of plenty is complicated by a profit system founded on scarcity.

Some of these developments would surprise John Stuart Mill, but he was not mistaken in one of his observations. In his *Principles of Political Economy* he wrote: "Self-help must be stimulated, not deadened by stifling dependence on a class of superiors, or on the state. The extraordinary growth of co-operation is one of the most cheering signs of modern times."

What would Mill say today of the fact that London Co-operative Society enrolls as many as one thousand new members in a week—in the words of a director, "with no stunt or campaign effort." It was this same director who commented: "I dare say you have learned while over here that there are some people in the movement on this side who are not so extreme as Dr. Warbasse seems to think."

"Too many are apt to make a battering ram out of the co-operative movement to force their way into other fields," the president of another society told me. "It is one thing wildly to wave the red flag, and it is another to quietly pursue our way, still making sure that we have our own political representation. It will never do to forget that it is our first duty to run this business so efficiently that we can keep ahead of our competitors."

A socialized outlook marked by individual intelligence and collective efficiency has built the British consumer movement.

This island of sanity flashes its light across a stormy sea to warn of shoals on which modern civilization may wreck itself. An age whose citizens place so much faith in speedy solutions and take their chief pleasure in the role of spectators must find a moral purpose in order to save itself. How to restore the old habits of participation and revive the sense of fulfilling some objective outside and beyond the preservation or extension of political governments? Lord Williams makes this answer:

"Let there be a rekindling of that faith—faith in the capacity of ordinary men and women to do for themselves in a co-operative way those things which satisfy their consumer and domestic requirements. The potentialities of the Movement are as great today as at any period in its history, and we can look to the future with optimism and without fear, if we work together to advance its principles, and refuse to sacrifice integrity of purpose for expediency and opportunism."

# BOOK LIST

Books obtainable from the Co-operative Union, Manchester 4, England:

*British Co-operative Movement in a Socialist Society*, by G. D. H. Cole. Allen and Unwin, 1942.

*Century of Co-operation*, by G. D. H. Cole. Co-operative Union, 1944.

*Congress Report.* Co-operative Union (annual).

*Consumers' Co-operation in Great Britain*, by A. M. Carr-Saunders et al. Allen and Unwin, 1942.

*Consumers' Democracy.* Co-operative Wholesale Society, 1951.

*Co-operation: What It Means and How It Works*, by Margaret Digby, O.B.E. Longmans Green, 1947.

*The Co-operative Movement in a Collectivist Economy* (policy statement). Co-operative Union, 1949.

*The Co-operative Movement in Labour Britain*, edited by N. Barou, Ph.D. Gollanc, 1948.

*Co-operative Statistics.* Co-operative Union (annual).

*Co-operators' Year Book.* Co-operative Productive Federation, Leicester (annual).

*Dividend Policy.* Co-operative Union, 1953.

*England Cradle of Co-operation*, by S. R. Elliott. Faber and Faber, 1937.

*Financial Policy.* Co-operative Union (annual).

*Handbook to the Industrial and Provident Societies Acts, 1893–1928*, by R. Southern. Co-operative Union, 1947.

*History of Co-operation*, by G. J. Holyoake. Fisher Unwin, 1906.

*History and Development of Wholesale Co-operation in Scotland.* Scottish CWS, 1953.

*Housing Associations.* National Federation of Housing Societies.

*New History of the Co-operative Wholesale Society,* by Percy Redfern. CWS, 1938.

*Rochdale Pioneers,* by W. H. Brown. Co-operative Union, 1944.

*Social Ownership* (policy statement). Co-operative Union, 1953.

*Towards the Co-operative Commonwealth,* by T. W. Mercer. Co-operative Press, 1936.

*World Co-operative Movement,* by Margaret Digby, O.B.E. Hutchinson, 1948.

Books published in the United States:

*Cooperation as a Way of Peace,* by James P. Warbasse. Harper & Brothers, 1939.

*Cooperative Democracy,* by James P. Warbasse. Harper & Brothers, 1947.

*A Cooperative Economy: A Study of Democratic Economic Movements,* by Benson Y. Landis. Harper & Brothers, 1943.

*The Cooperative Movement and Some of Its Problems,* by Paul Hubert Casselman. Philosophical Library, 1952.

*The Cooperatives Look Ahead,* by Jerry Voorhis. Public Affairs Committee, 1952.

*The Decline and Rise of the Consumer,* by Horace M. Kallen. Packard and Company, 1945.

*Fundamentals of Consumer Cooperation,* by V. S. Alanne. Co-operative Publishing Association, 1941.

*Masters of Their Own Destiny,* by M. M. Coady. Harper & Brothers, 1939.

*Organization and Management of Consumers' Cooperatives.* Bureau of Labor Statistics, 1951.

*Ourselves, Inc.,* by Leo R. Ward. Harper & Brothers, 1945.

*Sweden: The Middle Way,* by Marquis Childs. Yale University Press, 1947.

# INDEX

# INDEX

*Set in Linotype Janson*
*Format by Marguerite Swanton*
*Manufactured by The Haddon Craftsmen, Inc.*
*Published by* HARPER & BROTHERS, *New York*